Putting Taxpayers First

Putting Taxpayers First

A Blueprint for Victory in the Garden State

by Mayor Steve Lonegan

Foreword by Seth Grossman, Esq.

Kudzu Media, North Augusta

First Paperback Edition, September 2008

Copyright © 2007 by Steve Lonegan
www.lonegan.com

Published by Kudzu Media, North Augusta, SC
www.kudzumedia.com
Originally published by Kudzu Media in 2007.

Foreword copyright © 2007 by Seth Grossman, Esq.

Printed in the United States of America

Cover designed by Paul Horuzy

Hardcover Edition Library of Congress Control Number: 2007934731

Lonegan, Steve
        Putting Taxpayers First: A Blueprint for Victory in the Garden State
        / Steve Lonegan
        p. cm.
        ISBN 978-0-9729292-3-3
        1. Politics - New Jersey. 2. Conservatism – New Jersey.

Dedicated to the taxpayers of New Jersey

Contents

Foreword

In New Jersey, we are identified by the nearest exit on the Jersey Turnpike or Garden State Parkway. I'm from a relaxed South Jersey shore town near Parkway Exit 30. Steve Lonegan is mayor of Bogota, one of dozens of New York suburbs crowded around Exit 159.

Our backgrounds seem as far apart as our exit numbers. My grandparents were Jews. Mayor Lonegan's were Irish and Italian Catholics. I had no talent or interest in sports, while Steve Lonegan started on his College football team. After college, I went to law school and started working as a lawyer as soon as I graduated. I went on to become an Atlantic City Councilman and Atlantic County Freeholder before settling in as a radio talk show host. Steve Lonegan built a successful retail and manufacturing business and was then elected to three terms as mayor of the heavily Democrat town of Bogota, where his record on cutting spending and keeping tax increases below the rate of inflation is second to none in New Jersey.

Steve Lonegan and I came together in 2000. In that year, "Republican" Governor Christie Todd Whitman and a "Republican" legislature agreed to borrow $8.6 billion for new schools in "poor" districts throughout the state.

I had problems with that. First, $8.6 billion was

a lot of money, and Governor Whitman had already put the state heavily into debt. Second, big chunks of that money were earmarked for lavish new schools in districts like Ocean City, one of the richest in the state. Third and most important, these "Republicans" planned to borrow this money without voter approval - something clearly forbidden by our state constitution.

I complained, but Steve Lonegan acted. Lonegan raised enough funds from around the state to mount a first class legal challenge. He inspired me and hundreds of others to write checks for that cause. Two years later, New Jersey's Supreme Court shocked the state. It ruled that the legislature could ignore the constitution and borrow money without the vote of the people - if they used a simple loophole. The New Jersey Supreme Court said it was okay for the legislature to create a dummy corporation and let that dummy do the borrowing. The high court also said it was okay for the state legislature to "voluntarily" raise state taxes and reimburse that dummy corporation every year for the next 30 years.

With no constitutional limitation, the new Democrat Governor Jim McGreevey borrowed and spent the $8.6 billion in record time in what turned out to be the most wasteful and corrupt program in New Jersey's sorry history. Then Governor McGreevey and the Democrat-controlled legislature used the same gimmick to borrow billions more without public votes with the tobacco settlement and highway gasoline taxes.

Now, current Democrat Governor Jon Corzine is about to take that loophole even further with a proposed "monetization" and "leverage" of the Parkway, Turnpike, Interstate 80 and the Pulaski Skyway! So far, New Jersey Republicans have either joined in this borrowing and spending spree, or given half-hearted and ineffective opposition.

In this book, Mayor Lonegan patiently explains

how New Jersey changed from the   high-tech, high growth, no-debt, low tax state it was in the 1960s to the infamous target of late night TV comics it is today.

In many ways, Steve Lonegan's book reads like a history of 18th Century medicine. Back then, doctors treated sick patients by removing their "bad" blood. The sicker their patients got, the more blood these quacks would remove. Eventually, many of them, including George Washington, died from loss of blood - not from the disease.

In *Putting Taxpayers First*, Steve Lonegan explains how leading Republicans, Democrats, union leaders, and university professors in New Jersey all agree that more laws, debt, spending, and taxes will cure New Jersey's problems. And he shows how these treatments during the past 40 years have made things in New Jersey far worse instead of better.

For example, Chapter 3 carefully documents how New Jersey political and academic leaders successfully lobbied for higher state taxes on income, sales, and business to "cut" local real estate taxes. Although new money from these state taxes poured into local towns and school districts, local real estate tax hikes increased even more.

Just over forty years ago, New Jersey had the third highest property taxes in the country. But we had no sales tax, income tax, lottery, or casinos, and business taxes were a fourth of what they are today. Today we have all those taxes, and our sales, income, and business taxes are now among the highest in the nation. Yet real estate taxes went up even more and are now the highest in the nation! This book points out that these 40 years of new taxes and tax hikes did nothing to improve public education - the main recipient of the new money.

In *Putting Taxpayers First*, Steve Lonegan also shows current plans by Democrat Governor Jon Corzine to increase state debt, "monetize" state toll roads, consolidate small towns into big ones, and force all new homes to be built in high density "smart growth" areas that threaten to make things even worse.

But Steve Lonegan is not a complainer. *Putting Taxpayers First* presents some surprisingly simple and workable solutions. This revealing book explains how New Jersey citizens in the past applied now forgotten principles of liberty and personal responsibility to create opportunities for wealth for almost anyone willing to work for it.

Steve Lonegan reminds us that New Jersey's motto, "Liberty and Prosperity," has real meaning. Where there is liberty and justice for all, everyone can have a prosperous and comfortable life. He reminds us that when the words of our state motto meant something, so did the words written on the Trenton railroad bridge - "Trenton Makes. The World Takes."

I hope every candidate and elected official in New Jersey reads *Putting Taxpayers First* from cover to cover. Although the book gives New Jersey Republicans detailed instructions on how they can again become relevant, he also reminds New Jersey Democrats of how our state also prospered in the past when their party was in control. At that time, Democrats and Republicans alike respected our constitution and understood and applied New Jersey's motto: "Liberty and Prosperity."

Seth Grossman, Esq.
WIBG Radio Talk Show Host
Former Atlantic City Councilman
Former Atlantic County Freeholder

Introduction

Election Day 2006 saw the national Republican Party fall to minority status. The party that twelve years earlier had won a heady victory, taking control of the House of Representatives for the first time in decades with a vision of conservative leadership, had lost control in a humiliating defeat. To many it seemed the end of an era. But was it?

Republicans won in 1994 by mobilizing a conservative nation's voters against the politically correct liberal excesses of Bill Clinton and the liberals in Congress. Voters chose conservative leadership that ran on a platform of reducing the size of government and restoring individual freedom, personal responsibility, and Constitutional law.

For conservatives, 1994 marked a chance to implement the policy changes necessary to turn our nation away from an expanding welfare state and slow the continuous growth of a federal government increasingly determined to interfere in every aspect of our lives. Voters were excited.

The debilitating governmental shift toward entitlement that began with Franklin D. Roosevelt and metamorphosed after World War II into a "cradle to grave" government mentality was waning.

The Reagan Revolution overtook American politics like a juggernaut, realigning entire agencies, albeit not overnight. With the 1994 victory, conservative-thinking Americans were confident our country was back on track to becoming that "Shining City on a Hill" Reagan had illustrated so brilliantly. New Jersey helped elect President Reagan twice and George Bush Sr. to his first term with solid majorities. A year before Newt Gingrich and the 1994 conservative revolutionaries took over Congress, New Jersey elected a candidate for Governor who campaigned as a tax-cutting conservative. That candidate was Christine Todd Whitman.

Governor Whitman's election gave New Jersey conservatives hope. Although she had long been identified with the party's so-called "moderate" wing that worked with liberal Democrats to raise taxes and spending, her campaign had a markedly conservative tilt. She was endorsed by leading pro-life conservative legislators. The hallmark of her campaign was a Reaganesque across-the-board tax cut put together by conservative economists Steve Forbes and Larry Kudlow.

Conservatives were encouraged further after Governor Whitman's tax cuts passed through the legislature, whose Republican numbers had zoomed to an overwhelming majority in 1991 after Governor Jim Florio's backbreaking income, sales and other tax hikes.

But the honeymoon ended quickly. Governor Whitman first went to war with cultural conservatives; then went further by pushing a politically-correct liberal agenda that included more spending and affirmative action programs more radical than that of any other state in the union.

In 1995, Republicans lost seats in the New Jersey state legislative elections and again in 1997 when 7 percent of voters – mostly conservatives – backed third-party candidates for Governor. Governor Whitman won re-election with just 46 percent of the vote, a number that soon became the norm for Republicans running in the Garden State.

Rather than understanding the message from the 1997 elections – that Republicans should act and govern like Republicans – Governor Whitman moved away from her conservative base and launched what was at the time the biggest expansion of state government in New Jersey history. Governor Whitman embraced the views of the radical left across the board, even ordering her State Republican Chairman to send a memo to GOP activists asking them to join the environmentally extremist Sierra Club.

In her second inaugural address, Governor Whitman endorsed the creation of a host of liberal social engineering programs. She included mandatory, taxpayer-funded pre-kindergarten in urban school districts, which was destined to spread to the suburbs and pave the way for Governor Jon Corzine's call for "universal pre-K." She also endorsed "smart growth" policies designed to turn suburbs into cities and even abandoned tax cutting – calling for a hike in the state's gasoline tax.

The *Star Ledger* said: "The Christie Whitman of 30 percent tax cuts and shrunken government was missing-in-action yesterday as she was sworn into her second term as Governor. Instead, an expansive Whitman was suggesting ways to spend money - to rebuild the state's cities, add mass transit lines, save open space, invest more in county colleges, eliminate traffic congestion and even build bike paths."

Soon-to-be Governor Jim McGreevey summed up this abandonment of conservative principles by saying, "It was a tremendous speech… The Governor gave it better than I could."[1]

---

1   Wald, David; Whitman's Bold Plan, The Star-Ledger, January 21, 1998

I knew, as I sat in the audience in the New Jersey Performing Arts Center that day, the Republican Party was doomed to lose control of New Jersey. Grand Old Party leaders had abandoned the conservative principles that brought them to power. The GOP wasn't so grand anymore.

The failure to live up to the principles the GOP had staked its reputation on is the root cause of the sudden shift from a state with a Republican Governor, Senate, and Assembly, to a Democratic stronghold that many people believe the GOP has little hope of regaining. Within a short period of time New Jersey underwent a precipitous change to become what is now considered by many to be a state that can't be won by a conservative candidate – or for that matter any Republican.

The slide continued further in 1999 when Republicans lost even more Assembly seats and the final blow came in 2001 when the Whitman-backed candidate for Governor actually lost the Republican Primary. This party split combined with exploding budgets and debt in the final Whitman years and new legislative redistricting, where Governor Whitman's "Republican" Chief Justice cast the tie breaking vote, led to Democrats taking over the State Assembly and engineering a tie in the State Senate.

Nonetheless, her legacy lives on. With a tie in the State Senate, Republican leaders refused to maintain party discipline, giving now Governor McGreevey key votes on tax increases and even bigger liberal spending schemes. They then scratched their heads as the GOP lost even more seats in the 2003 elections and again in 2005 when the GOP gubernatorial nominee rejected conservative principles.

On the day Christie Whitman was elected, Republicans held 27 of 40 State Senate seats. In 2007 they have just 18. The situation has become even worse in the Assembly, where Republicans have dropped from 58 of 80 to only 30 seats in 2007.

Unless Republicans go back to their roots by standing with conservatives rather than against us, the New Jersey GOP will continue to wither, and any hope of saving New Jersey from the Corzine-Codey-McGreevey-Menendez-Lautenberg crowd will be gone forever.

The Republican losses in 2006 on the national level can be traced to the same pattern. The GOP, which was once a bulwark against big-spending and liberal big-government, has become the party of big spending and big government under George W. Bush.

The 2006 defeats were not a defeat for conservatism, but a rejection of the big-government policies represented by No Child Left Behind and the spending excesses embodied in the infamous Alaskan "Bridge to Nowhere."

Republicans can win again in New Jersey – and in America – and this book is a blueprint for how it can and will be done. The answer is simple: Embrace our conservative principles rather than hide from them, and, most of all, put taxpayers first.

Chapter One

A Definition of Insanity

*"Insanity: doing the same ineffective thing again and
again expecting a different result."*
--Albert Einstein

Casting aspersions is easy, especially when the
target is the Democratic Party and its failed liberal policies. History has shown again and again the direct cause
and effect of taxes on economic productivity (specifically,
lower taxes mean a stronger economy, higher taxes mean
a weaker economy), yet year after year, decade after decade, the liberals keep getting it wrong. Republicans took
a drubbing in the mid-term elections of 2006, but this was
not in any way a referendum on conservative principles,
but rather our leaders' unwillingness to govern by them.

American history in the past 60 years is rife with
examples of liberals growing government and appropri-
ating freedom that belongs to the people, but nowhere
are the devastating effects of such liberal policies so na-
kedly on display as they are in the state of New Jersey.

In just a few years a syndicate of power-hungry,
liberal bureaucrats have taken a thriving economy and

driven it into the ground, amassing huge debts and running roughshod over the rights of the people and the state constitution along the way. And they're getting away with it because the ultra-liberal New Jersey Supreme Court is on their side.

For almost 200 years New Jersey supported a boom economy. Planted between Philadelphia and New York City, increasing numbers of workers from the city, looking to escape rising taxes and crime rates found suburban havens in New Jersey as communities expanded to meet the demand. With the expansion of the railroad system, farms gave way to mansions that gave way to housing subdivisions. People migrated from densely populated, more-expensive urban areas to suburban settings in droves, as infrastructure continued to open up more of the state.

By the mid-20th century, because so many New Jersey residents worked high-paying jobs in New York, the state had the highest average family income in the United States. These former New York residents liked the smaller government and lower taxes that had been the hallmark of the economic expansion in the state. By the early 1960s New Jersey was one of the only holdout states that managed to escape both a sales and income tax.

In 1966, Democratic Governor Richard J. Hughes managed to wrestle a 3 percent sales tax through the legislature, taking the first halting steps toward runaway government expansion. The sales tax was hiked four years later to 5 percent and New Jersey got a lottery, both with the promise of lower property taxes. A state income tax was added in 1976.

As is always the case, with the increase in revenue came a commensurate growth in government power. Money was lavished on education and programs for low-income citizens in the big cities, with very little positive result to show for the spending. Government spending spiraled upward out of control as liberal leaders with slim accountability indulged in pet projects and graft. In his seminal article on the stranglehold of unions in New Jersey, City Journal reporter Steven Malanga observed:

> "Two interlocking forces drove the spending: first, the rise of powerful public-sector unions that pushed effectively for higher pay and benefits, bloating municipal and school budgets and blocking needed reforms not just in cities but across the state; second, the growth in Jersey cities of a new kind of political machine that diverted federal and state urban aid into political favors and patronage, wasting billions on useless and often crooked programs, and turning the cities into expensive wards of the state."[1]

Having a little tax is like being a little bit pregnant. Eventually, the extra revenue gives birth to a 300 pound money-guzzling baby getting fatter and fatter on the backs of the taxpayers. Everyone with the integrity to say "That's a fat baby!" is shouted down, threatened or bought.

Buying influence has a long and notorious history in New Jersey. By the time of the race riots in the late 1960s, the big cities were in the grip of Mob bosses, a power base only dislodged when federal prosecutors turned up the heat. Unfortunately, the men who filled the power vacuum were little better than the criminals they replaced. Over three decades, a long string of probes of city corruption hounded and took down city officials, councilmen and even a few mayors.

Fed up with the endless corruption and egregious

---

1   Malanga, Steven; The Mob That Whacked New Jersey, City Journal, Spring 2006

squandering of taxpayer money, workers ceded more and more power to the unions, hoping that collectively they could wrest some control of their own futures out of the hands of the thugs in office. In the same article, Malanga describes a particularly flagrant example:

> "Newark's teachers' union, for example, used Gibson's legal woes to seize control of the schools from the mayor and deliver it to a school board - which the union, with more than 4,000 voting members, could easily elect. The result: a long period of school-system misman-agement and fraud, documented in a damn-ing 1994 state investigation, which culminated in state takeover of the system the next year."[2]

New Jersey could learn from the Communist ex-periments. Communists in the Soviet Union experienced the wonders of socialism first hand over the space of almost 70 years, and a stark list of realities emerged across the social landscape in Mother Russia:

- No matter how hard they try to treat all citizens equally, the people in power still end up more wealthy than the average Joe;
- Governments cannot do anything better than pri-vate citizens, except raise a military and carry out matters of civil justice;
- Without a free market, workers lose the will to excel, productivity lags, and quality suffers;
- Without financial motivation, the only way to im-pel citizens is through coercion, ergo socialism leads inexorably toward tyranny.

Capitalism is the only system that produces last-

---

2   Ibid

ing prosperity. The market works, not because one philosophy is superior to the other, but because people are, by nature, driven to achieve. Even altruistic people operate under the bridle of enlightened self-interest. Capitalism works because it takes human nature into account, allowing people to excel if they wish. Socialism does not. Everyone is treated the same and superior performance and thinking are discouraged.

A shining example of this principle comes out of China. It seems there was a bicycle company that had always suffered from lackluster performance. The leaders of the company had set a daily quota of 1,000 bicycles and the workers consistently came in short by several hundred. Every day the workers produced 500, 600, 550, bicycles, but never anywhere near the target number. One day as an experiment, the leaders told the workers for one day only, they could keep any bicycles they made over the quota. The workers produced 2000 bicycles in one day. The market works.

In Russia, toilets don't work, water quality is often poor, environmental violations are ubiquitous. The standard of living for the general populace is consistently at shockingly low levels for an industrialized nation. Of course, it's only surprising if you think humans respond well to being told no individual is intrinsically valuable.

The market works because we believe every living, breathing person has the potential to be more than they are today. Comparison after comparison proves we are right. With such a sweeping example of the abject failure of socialism in practice in the Soviet Union, it is dumbfounding that segments of our own populace continue to allow their leaders to govern to the left.

It is not surprising New Jersey has suffered a crushing exodus of citizens to less hostile environs. The population of Newark has been nearly cut in half, but even so there are fewer jobs and crime is on the rise. As people flow out of urban areas into surrounding communities, the thugs in power keep looking for ways to put the bite on them anyway. For example, by pushing through legislation like the Abbott Decision, which forces suburban communities to foot the bill for bloated programs by mandating that each school district be able to spend as much as the state's most affluent school districts. The skyrocketing costs of the mandate are of course paid for through statewide tax increases.

The only downside to "the market works" is for those who make poor decisions and suffer the consequences. Historically, New Jersey has held a top spot among the 50 states when it comes to cutting edge technologies. Much of our past economic success, quality of life, and standard of living is attributable to that fact. But times they are a-changin.' A recent report for Rutgers University by James Hughes and Joseph Seneca made the following observation:

"... [R]ecent years have seen signs of an erosion of New Jersey's once-unique advanced economic assets. There have also been subtle but significant shifts in the state's employment growth patterns signaling that the state's position as an economic leader is beginning to slip away. Key parts of the core economy - including the state's unique concentrations of technology-based economic specializations... have started to contract."[3]

The Rutgers report goes on to point out that since 2000, New Jersey has suffered a disturbing shift in the distribution of high-paying service or manufacturing jobs and low-paying service jobs, and a sharp increase

---

3   James W. Hughes and Joseph J. Seneca, Rutgers Regional Report: New Jersey's New Economy Growth Challenges, Issue Paper 25, July 2006

of taxpayer-funded government jobs over private-sector jobs. Coupled with a rather abrupt drop in technology-based industries as compared to the nation, the trend becomes more nettlesome as all-important economic indicators continue to slide.

During the 1980s and 1990s New Jersey's economy was substantially transformed from a declining manufacturing-based paradigm to an information-driven paradigm. The future looked very bright, but on the heels of a national recession, with waste and corruption permeating the highest levels of government, and a tax structure hostile to both business and citizens, since 2000 bad government policies have managed to erode most of our economic reasons for optimism.

Contributing to the problem is the fact that increasing numbers of New Jersey economic institutions are being bought by organizations outside the state, effectively transferring control of those companies beyond our borders.

According to Hughes and Seneca it took 32 years (until 2001) for manufacturing employment to shrink by 50 percent, but it only took 9 years (since 1995) for high-technology wired telecommunications to drop by half, made more troubling by the fact that these were high-paying jobs at nearly double the industry average.

Near the end of the century, the rate at which government employment in New Jersey expanded was moderate, with new jobs occurring more dominantly in the private sector. After 2000, however, that trend flipped alarmingly, with a staggering increase in public-sector jobs, effectively reducing the jobless rate on the backs of taxpayers. Thanks to the comparatively high level of affluence in the state, those backs are pretty strong even now, but they won't take this kind of punishment forever. The longer New Jersey stays on this course of socialistic income redistribution, cronyism, power consolidation, and market manipulation, the less likely it is that this course can be changed sufficiently to avoid economic and social disaster.

With over 40 percent of the total state budget siphoning back to county and municipal agencies and school districts in the form of aid programs, cries of "compassion" disguise the real agenda and effect: central government control of all education (and everything else, for that matter).

Witness the appalling court-ordered effort to rehabilitate the decrepit urban school systems by bypassing voter approval to create a bonding authority, a constitutional end-around sanctioned by the highest court in the state. Now taxpayers across the state have to foot more than 80 percent of the education bill for the inner cities, with no political say in the matter. And the unions are only compounding the problem.

Formed ostensibly to protect the rights of workers, unions inevitably devolve into greedy power centers, made more corrupt because once they wield enough power, their leaders don't answer to anyone but themselves, so the propensity toward despotic thinking and behavior is more pronounced. Once they sink their fangs into a source of money or power, like a pit bull they clamp their jaws shut and won't let go.

The New Jersey Education Association (NJEA) recently spearheaded a $300,000 ad campaign opposing an effort led by taxpayers to call a constitutional convention to attack the tax problem. A couple of years ago the state legislature was working on a bill to try to corral school spending by putting a cap on it of 2.5 percent, or the rate of inflation, whichever was less. The NJEA strong-armed the politicians and succeeded in having the word "less" changed to "greater."

Another political cartel, the Communication Workers of America (CWA), claiming to represent the interests of government employees, ran radio ads heavily backing a $1 billion hike in the tax burden on New Jersey businesses, proclaiming with self-righteous indignation that companies needed to pay their "fair share." This is pure, unadulterated, socialist income redistribution alive and well in the hearts of our union leadership. They are committed, mobilized and will not relinquish their stranglehold on the state without a bitter fight. It will take courage to wage the battle against the unions, but wage it conservatives must.

Only free-market thinking will save our state. The Rutgers Report said it best, "...the state needs to create and sustain an economic and entrepreneurial environment conducive to the growth of new, high-knowledge content, high-value-added businesses."[4]

Translation: Trenton must return to the principles of a free-market economy. Our politicians must put an end to expensive income redistribution schemes draped in the guise of social equality. Our leaders need to learn again what it means to have integrity, what it feels like to do something because it's right, not because they can pay off political debts with the additional revenue.

Our state has been so wealthy that the economic disaster on our doorstep has crept ever nearer without most people noticing the seriousness of the situation. Policymakers and the electorate have been lulled into a false sense of security, dogged by a Pollyanna belief that somehow it will all work itself out. Our lawmakers blithely keep trying to stay the course. A revisit to the definition of insanity at the beginning of this chapter would not be amiss. At best, many of the political power brokers in our state are ignorant of human nature and historical fact; at worst, they care only for their own welfare, and will sit fat and happy on the economic ashes of our state, unless the general populace rises up with grim

---

4   Ibid

determination and says, "Enough."

The economic challenges facing New Jersey are complicated, and the answers will not be easy, but we can say with considerable confidence that liberal economic policy is not going to dig us out of this hole. Grossly overspending and then making up the budget shortfall with higher taxes is not going to stabilize our economy. Our leaders need to know that we know there's a problem, and we know that they don't have a plan to fix it, and if they don't come up with one on which we agree, we're just fed up enough to take over the helm and steer the ship into more prosperous waters ourselves.

I leave the final word to Hughes and Seneca:

"New Jersey needs to pay sustained attention to its economic development policies and its business environment to recapture its former comparative advantages. No less than the future economic well being of the state is at stake."[5]

---

5   Ibid

Chapter Two

The Millstone Around Our Necks

"The politicians don't just want your money. They want your soul. They want you to be worn down by taxes until you are dependent and helpless. When you subsidize poverty and failure, you get more of both."
--James Dale Davidson, National Taxpayers Union

New Jersey has the highest sales tax in the nation, the highest property taxes in the country, and the worst income tax structure of any state, while simultaneously being crushed under the nation's fastest growing state debt. It is all made manifest in the fastest growing total tax burden of all fifty states.

Not coincidentally, New Jersey is home to the most powerful and influential government employee labor unions in the United States, unions which are better understood as political cartels. Their arrogance is outrageous, the heavy-handed power they wield difficult to withstand, but it is within our control to turn things around. It will take political courage and stamina, and the iron will to see it through. To know where we're going, we have to understand where we've been, and one need only look across the Hudson River to delve into the lessons our particular history has to offer.

New York City has long stood as a bastion of urban wealth and industry, yet the Big Apple was nearly brought to its knees in the 1970s when the damage wrought by decades of city worker unions hammering away for higher wages and costly benefits nearly drove the city into bankruptcy.

Generations of New York politicians eager to have union support on Election Day sold out to union bosses, regardless of the long-term and even short-term impact on the city's financial strength. City managers caved to demands for higher salaries that began to outdistance those of equivalent private-sector workers. Funds were diverted from maintenance and capital needs to feed the ever-growing hunger of the empowered government-worker unions.

What else can be expected from politicians eager to hold on to their prestigious positions when government-employee unions could mobilize thousands of their members on Election Day to get out the vote? These politicians, like many of those in New Jersey, lacked the courage and conviction to take on these political cartels and risk winning or losing.

To paraphrase the old saying, "Those who do not learn from the past are condemned to repeat it," and every day New Jersey's elected officials prove the saying is true. New Jersey's government-worker unions have emerged as the most powerful political force in the state. The NJEA is the largest donor of campaign funds in the state, giving to politicians on both sides of the partisan aisle who will support their agenda. Combined with the Communications Workers of America and other government employee unions they represent the only growth sector for unions in an already-bloated government.

But are these organizations really unions in the traditional sense? I don't think so. The traditional labor unions formed during the industrial revolution served to protect workers from large, centralized capital and industrial barons willing to drive down salaries to the bottom as long as a steady supply of new workers flowing in from the agricultural economy were willing to tolerate lower wages and poor working conditions.

As a believer in individual liberty I support the right of workers to unionize and negotiate for better wages directly with those paying their salaries. This system has worked when labor unions were reasonable and understood the need of management to be competitive. It has failed miserably in cases where union demands have forced companies to relocate in order to find lower wages and remain competitive in the free market.

Unionized government workers are far different. They are not protecting themselves from large central ized capital or industry barons. They don't need to bargain collectively for a fair wage. So, who are they protecting themselves against? It can only be the taxpayer. Ultimately, it is the taxpayer who is paying the salary, not the politicians.

Traditional unions negotiate directly with those paying their salaries. Government unions negotiate with those who take citizens' money and then negotiate how to spend it for their political advantage.

This simple fact drastically alters the intention of those negotiating for the government. No intelligent person would try to purchase a home by handing a bag of cash to a real estate broker and trusting him to negotiate a good deal, especially if the seller had the muscle to get the broker fired, yet this is how the unions expect taxpayers to allow the government to run.

Truth be told, New Jersey's government unions are not unions at all. They are political cartels whose sole purpose is to place enormous amounts of political power in the hands of union bosses and use that power to exercise political influence. One of the consequences of this political power is forcing employee wages beyond what taxpayers can afford.

The Associated Press reported in a November 22, 2006 article by Linda A. Johnson that for the first time equivalent jobs in the state government compared to the private sector now paid more than the private sector as well as offering superior benefits and secure retirement.

New Jersey taxpayers are far from being greedy industrial barons, quite the opposite. Our state taxpayers have proven to be generous to a fault, regularly passing public referendums for new debt and relying on elected officials who tell us how important it is to "invest" in our state's future.

Today public opinion is changing, and changing rapidly. Taxpayers are recognizing the destructive effect the growth of central government and its enormous cost is having on our economy. With the union bosses driving the train, our state is on track to a train wreck that would make the financial conditions New York City faced in the 1970s seem like a blip.

A primary tenet of conservatism holds that power corrupts, and more power has a correspondingly larger corrupting influence. This is true in every human endeavor, religion, business, sports, and the entertainment industry, but is most insidious when the power coalesces around a desire to help people. Gathering millions to do the work of God is a beautiful thing; gathering millions so you can play God is socialism.

The trade unions in our country sprang from a reasonable desire by workers that they work in decent conditions, receive a decent wage, and be able to take care of their families. Since Cain killed Abel people have been trying to eat the "other guy's" lunch. In the middle ages they called it war. In the industrial revolution they called it business, but the fact remains that one of the ways to maximize profits is to cut employee wages and benefits, and when management allows avarice to get the upper hand over common sense, the workers lose.

As industry grew in America, sweatshops emerged as a cheap form of production. These were often filthy, makeshift garment factories in grimy tenements where workers worked 80 hour weeks with meager wages.

I come from a family of union workers. My grandparents who came here from Italy in the early part of the century were International Ladies Garment Workers Union (ILGWU) members, working hard in the downtown Manhattan garment district. My Irish grandfather was a member of the International Brotherhood of Electrical Workers (IBEW), arguably the most socialistic of all the East Coast unions.

The weekend dinner table with my family was filled with talk of union issues, especially at election time. My Italian grandparents, fiercely independent after escaping the fascist regime of Mussolini, were not going to be told who to vote for by the union bosses and spat on the union newspaper. This was not the case on the IBEW side. Grandpa Lonegan was a loyal soldier who voted the union guidelines, which were of course always the Democratic column.

Despite differences of opinion about the union's political agenda, the fact is these unions were real unions and served a clear purpose in representing the interests of their members in standing up to oftentimes corrupt management. The public employee political cartels are an insult to the tradition and value of real labor unions.

You can only push a person so far before he or she rises up and revolts. Within the American Labor Movement, understanding that many soldiers make an army, workers quickly learned that they were much stronger as a group, and trade unions were born as a means to improve working conditions. One need not look far to discover whether they were successful or not. Now it is management that works 80 hour weeks, while the rank and file works 40. Minimum wage, the Occupational Safety and Health Administration, Workers' Compensation, and numerous labor laws are in place to help ensure the livelihood of the average worker and keep the workplace tolerable and safe.

When unions behave themselves and honestly pursue reasonable wages and benefits, the system works. Unfortunately, mobs on the whole are not an overly analytical bunch, and for many unionized workers, as soon as they realize they can "vote a benefit from the treasury" by demanding higher wages and more benefits, company owners start to feel the bite. What these workers don't realize is that the money has to come from somewhere, and it isn't going to come out of management's pocket. A textbook example of this is found in the Paterson silk strikes of the early 20th century.

"Skilled workmen, proud of their craft and aggressive in the pursuit of justice as they conceived it, were central to the rise of Paterson – and to its fall. Their old independent habits, their constant strikes, and their many victories were costly to the silk manufacturers. By resisting with all their strength and wisdom the tendency of capitalism to turn improvements in machinery against them by lowering the value of their labor, the skilled male weavers forced the flight of capital from Paterson."[1]

1   Golin, Steve; The Fragile Bridge: Paterson Silk Strike 1913; Temple University Press; November 5, 1992

When workers make unreasonable demands for more money, they hurt the bottom line and hurt the profitability of the company, which damages company performance. Everybody loses, and all for a few cents more on a paycheck.

New Jersey started out as a safe haven for business owners who were fed up with the increasing regulation and taxation happening in the major urban areas like New York and Philadelphia. Land was cheap and taxes low; as a consequence, industry thrived and our state had a steady inflow of higher income people and jobs during the economic boom in the last century.

Unfortunately for the general populace, unions and socialist politicians make great bedfellows. Unions can swing an election in favor of a politician friendly to their cause, and politicians can push legislation that benefits the unions.

A glaring case in point are so-called Project Labor Agreements, Governor Jim McGreevey's Executive Order One, which effectively forced counties, municipalities, and school boards to pay artificially high union wages for virtually any government construction or renovation project.

The payback comes in the form of millions of dollars from labor unions directly into the coffers of politicians, mostly Democrats but including some "moderate" Republicans as well. This kind of largesse has encouraged politicians with a liberal bent to become ever more reckless in their tax-and-spend policies, to the point that Malanga called New Jersey a cautionary example of how to cripple a thriving state:

> "Increasingly muscular public-sector unions have won billions in outlandish benefits and wages from compliant officeholders. A powerful public education cartel has driven school spend-

ing skyward, making Jersey among the nation's biggest education spenders, even as student achievement lags. Inept, often corrupt, politicians have squandered yet more billions wrung from suburban taxpayers, supposedly to uplift the poor in the state's troubled cities, which have nevertheless continued to crumble despite the record spending. To fund this extravagance, the state has relentlessly raised taxes on both residents and businesses, while localities have jacked up property taxes furiously."[2]

Ruthless and entrenched, the offending unions in New Jersey will not release their stranglehold on money and power without a fight. When an organization is strong and can bring a large voting bloc to the polls, politicians are understandably wary about taking them on. Republicans lost power after thinking they could bring the unions to their side, and continue to stay out of power because they are afraid to stand up to them.

No one should seriously expect Governor Jon Corzine to ever truly oppose public employee unions – notwithstanding his former girlfriend sitting across the table – just as they shouldn't have expected the same out of Governors Codey, McGreevey or Florio.

Corzine's promise to take on the union benefits problem and bring them in line with reality evaporated after the NJEA put several thousand union members in front of the State House on December 11, 2006. Most disturbing about this spectacle was the drama of Republican legislators jumping out in front of this crowd like lap dogs anxious to show their masters they had been properly trained and seeking a biscuit.

As long as the New Jersey Republican Party tol-

---

2   Malanga, Steven, The Mob That Whacked New Jersey, City Journal, Spring 2006

erates this wholesale sell-out of the principles of limited government and taxpayers, Republicans will never have control of New Jersey.

The scene at the Trenton rally emphasizes what I have stated all along: We don't have two parties in Trenton, we have one party and that is the party of big spenders. Worst of all, those big spenders are all under the control of the state union cartel.

The union leadership publicly lobbied that changes to benefits had to be negotiated "in good faith." In 2001 these unions used political pressure on the legislature to enhance their retirement benefits with a 9 percent increase. The union bosses worked the legislators to be sure they knew that if they wanted union support they were expected to support this extravagant increase.

Republicans and Democrats alike cowered under the pressure and capitulated much like the New York politicians of the 1960s and 1970s. Now, five years later with the state finances on the verge of collapse, the unions have decided that rolling back those enhancements is now "negotiable."

I never expected Governor Corzine to live up to his promise to take on the eight-hundred-pound gorilla, and not surprisingly he lived down any expectations of the sort. But voters did expect Republicans to stand up to unions and put taxpayers first. They failed and this is why Democrats run New Jersey today.

How do policymakers take on organized public employees and win? By standing tall and doing the job they were chosen by taxpayers to do. President Ronald Reagan showed all of us how. Just a few months after taking office, over 12,000 unionized Air Traffic Controllers in the PATCO union walked off the job during the busy season, hoping to disrupt airline transportation sufficiently to force the federal government to accede to their demands for a shorter work week and increased wages, a

$10,000 per-year, per-employee increase, no less.

President Reagan didn't back down. He demanded employees get back to work or be fired. The union thought he was bluffing, but Reagan knew the facts. Reagan knew the union contract had a no-strike clause and he enforced it. Reagan stood on principle and the public supported him. Substitute controllers were brought in and business carried on more or less as usual. Talks between PATCO and the FAA stalled and after one week, 11,000 air-traffic controllers received pink slips and 1,200 went back to work. The air was as safe as ever.

Reagan demonstrated the kind of unflinching courage that is necessary when unions cross the line. And the public revered him for it.

I had a similar experience in my town of Bogota. I came into office January 1996, taking over a town that had the highest tax rate in Bergen County and had experienced years of double-digit property tax increases. I told voters I would cut spending and stabilize taxes. This would be no easy trick, but my Republican council and I knew we had to succeed if we were going to bring economic stability to our community.

We rolled up our sleeves and went to work. We started day one by forfeiting our salaries the first year and promised not to take a salary until we had fulfilled our commitment to taxpayers. The mayor received a $1,800 a year stipend. Not much, but we hoped the gesture set an example and would pave the way for other department heads to find ways to cut spending.

Not so. Anyone who has had experience in government knows that budget cuts are always met with cries of alarm and bleak projections. Elected officials learn rapidly that there's always someone out there to whom even the most insignificant budget line item apparently is critical to our existence as a civilization. Cries from the loyal Democratic opposition about my irresponsible behavior notwithstanding, I managed to cut Bogota's budget the first year.

After that came the mythical eight-hundred-pound gorilla. I negotiated my first of four police contracts and quickly learned that negotiating with a public-sector bargaining unit was far more challenging than negotiating with a private-sector union. In these negotiations the forces of public perception and politics are more important than financial reality. I learned how rank-and-file union members would turn to the public for support if negotiations weren't going their way and how the opposition party disregards any effort to negotiate a fair contract in exchange for culling favor with the union. Both Republicans and Democrats are guilty of this abandoning of taxpayers. Police union negotiators know this and are adept at playing one party against another.

In 1996, a Bogota patrolman was earning a base salary of $56,033 and averaging an additional $10,000 in overtime. Benefits included full paid medical benefits so comprehensive they are no longer available in the private sector; unlimited sick days, thirteen holidays and four weeks vacation; plus, a range of smaller benefits. Additionally, an officer who retired after 25 years would receive 67 percent of the average of their highest two years salaries for life – with automatic cost of living increases.

During the decade prior to my administration the salaries of police in Bogota had grown far greater than the rate of inflation, widening the gap between the average household income in our community and average police salaries. The average household income in Bogota in 1996 was $36,000 according to the federal Census Bureau. When average salaries of government employees, including teachers, police and everyone else on the public payroll, exceed the average incomes of the taxpayers funding those salaries through local property taxes, it follows that the tax burden is going to take a larger and larger chunk of those taxpayers' income.

I believe a community should pay employees based on what it can afford and through fair negotiation with the employee via collective bargaining. As Mayor of Bogota I learned this is not the case in New Jersey. Rather, the final decision over government-employee salaries is made by a host of nameless, faceless bureaucrats from Trenton called the PERC (Public Employment Relations Commission) Board.

Under the state's "Binding Arbitration" law, contracts that cannot be resolved by the governing body and collective bargaining unit are remanded to this Board, which has gained a reputation for always siding with government employees. When negotiating on behalf of the police union, lawyers generally cite the salaries other towns are providing to police personnel as an argument for increased salaries. This creates a leap-frog effect, as a town's ability to pay seems to be no part of the PERC Board's determination since the Board assumes the town can always raise taxes.

It's no wonder local elected officials, usually well-meaning, low-paid community members, throw up their hands and simply capitulate, awarding lucrative contracts on a regular basis. The consequences of fighting back can be difficult, even on one's family. I know. I fought back.

Police negotiations in 1996 started out with a commitment to voters to get things under control. Our negotiating team wanted to keep any salary increases within the rate of inflation and thus begin to bring benefits in line with Bogota's fiscal reality and private-sector pay and benefits. We wanted to increase the co-pay on prescriptions from $2 to $5 for each prescription filled. The police union would have no part of it. They requested salary increases of 6 percent per-year for three years, or three times the inflation rate. This would drive taxes up for the next three years and was unconscionable.

I made Bogota's position clear and held the line. They made their position clear too and took it to the street, telling residents we were refusing to give the police a fair contract.   We took our negotiations to the PERC Board and lost. It is little wonder since the arbitrator appointed to our case was the one the police union requested. The PERC Board awarded the police a three-year contract with increases of 4.5 percent each year, or a salary increase of 14 percent over three years without any give backs.

This is when most governing bodies give up, but we refused to give up. Instead Bogota filed an appeal and the PERC review panel agreed the award was excessive and told the arbitrator to go back to the mediation table. The second time around it was made clear why this supposedly unbiased arbitrator was a police union favorite – he gave the police the same lucrative award and attempted to justify the numbers.

At this point any other governing body would have thrown in the towel. No one had ever appealed a PERC decision twice. We thought it was time to make history so we appealed the mediator's decision a second time and this time we won.

During this process the politics outside the negotiating room heated up to the boiling point. The police planted lawn signs all over town in purple and gold (the town colors) claiming "We Support the Bogota Police." The signs appeared on store windows and front lawns; even our supporters put up these banners in order to outwardly appease the other side. Council meetings were packed with residents wearing purple and gold "We Support Our Police" ribbons. After all, they said, these officers risk their lives every day and we should pay them whatever they ask.

How much they were being paid did not matter to this crowd. The fact that they were earning an average of

$20,000 more than a New York City police officer didn't matter either. In fact, many of those hysterical citizens who came to our meeting to advocate had no idea what the average cop was making and didn't care. It was pure politics. Just like the Republicans cheering on the Teachers' Union Rally in Trenton – it didn't matter how money was being spent. A noisy, emotional crowd was putting government employees, not taxpayers, first.

Despite the pressure, my administration held the line and stabilized taxes in Bogota. This contract was critical to achieving that goal. During the entire process, I was told I would be a one-term mayor. After all, no one could take on this union and get away with it. Nonetheless, I continued to stick to my commitment to put taxpayers first. The entire contract negotiating process took several years and by the time we had won the victory for taxpayers, it was time for my first re-election.

"We Support Our Police" signs were all over town. A gigantic "Support Bogota Police" message went up on a commercial billboard two weeks before the election. The Bogota police union was confident that I would go down in flaming defeat and some of my detractors had their chests puffed out just a little more on election day. My critics were disappointed, though. Our Republican team beat the Democrats with an overwhelming 23 points in 1999 and by 18 points in 2003. Not bad in a town that voted overwhelmingly for liberal Democrats Al Gore, John Kerry, Frank Lautenberg, Bob Menendez, Jon Corzine and Jim McGreevey. The lesson is clear: putting taxpayers first in policies and politics works.

Chapter Three

The Property Tax Relief Fraud

"A broad-based tax would mean the state is shifting from the old agrarian property tax and it would help relieve taxes of local property owners."
--Senate President William Ozzard, December 18, 1963

"Trenton is the problem not the solution."

That's the lesson New Jersey taxpayers have learned from forty years of false promises from the state's politicians.

Forty years ago, liberal politicians promised us that if we only had a 3 percent sales tax, the property tax problem would not only go away, but the revenues would allow a cut in the corporate business tax. At that time, the state budget was $876 million. New Jerseyans were told that if only our state could pass a 3 percent "temporary" sales tax it would solve the "property tax crisis." The tax would phase-out after building a surplus and could even be eliminated within a few years.

In 1965, New Jersey politicians were complaining

the state had the third highest per capita property taxes in the country. California ranked number one at $196 per capita, Massachusetts second at $173 and New Jersey coming in third at $172. New Jersey's total property tax bill for every town, county and school district: $1.4 billion. At the time New Jersey was one of only three states with no sales and income tax and virtually no state debt.

Obviously that's no longer the case today.

Forty years after politicians promised taxpayers an increase in state sales taxes would relieve the property tax burden, New Jersey today has the highest property taxes in the nation, the highest sales tax and the most progressive and destructive income tax in the country.

The reason is an out-of-control state government that cannot raise money fast enough to satisfy its voracious appetite for tax dollars.

The 1966 battle over the proposed sales tax was fierce. A sales tax was voted into law during the 1930s, only to be repealed by legislators reacting to angry voters. This time, teachers' union organizers packed the gallery with students wearing buttons "Better Education through Taxation."

They won with bipartisan support from prominent Republicans as well as Democrats. It came as no surprise to true conservatives that 3 percent was not enough in the end for cash-hungry politicians.

Just four years later, in 1970, the sales tax was hiked to 5 percent, and in spite of the sales tax hike and the creation of a state lottery that same year, demands for an income tax continued. Republican Governor William Cahill – a strong income tax supporter – appointed a "Blue Ribbon" committee to find ways to "cut property taxes."

Governor Cahill's hand-picked chairman, former State Senate President Harry Sears, who was instrumental in pushing through the lottery, called the income tax

"an integral part of tax reform and lower property taxes."

"We either have to equalize the property tax or
put some kind of limit on it," he said as he claimed that
senior citizens "are losing their homes because they cannot pay the taxes."

New Jerseyans would hear this claim again and
again in subsequent decades from politicians promising
the path to lower property taxes was raising state income
and sales taxes.

The income tax died under the Republicans but it
gained a new life when Democrats took over the legislature after Watergate. By 1976, Governor Brendan Byrne
and his solidly Democratic legislature pushed through
the income tax with another promise of property tax relief.

Byrne knew that voters demanded assurance from
Trenton politicians after the 1966 Sales Tax Fraud that
this new broad-based tax would solve the property tax
crisis once and for all. Byrne's income tax receipts would
go entirely towards a Property Tax Relief Fund. But the
Byrne plan didn't say whose property taxes were being
relieved.

I'll give you a hint, it wasn't suburban taxpayers.

Once in place, it was easy for both parties to "work
together" to raise sales taxes to 6 percent and top income
tax rates by 40 percent in 1982. In this sixteen-year period, state spending grew to just over $6 billion, more than
twice what it would have been if it remained constant
even with the record inflation of the Jimmy Carter years.
Whenever a politician pontificates about going to Trenton to "work together" remember what happens when
these guys cooperate. It always means more spending
and higher taxes.

The camel's back was broken again with Governor
Jim Florio's 1990 $2.8 billion tax hike that sparked a revolt

among New Jersey's over-taxed middle class.

Governor Florio doubled top income tax rates and raised sales taxes to 7 percent. But it was the more symbolic taxes – new taxes on everything from beer to telephone calls to gasoline to toilet paper – that spurred the biggest outcry. Democrats stood united as a bloc to push through these tax increases.

Incredibly, they were so deluded by the idea that voters actually wanted higher taxes in exchange for the vague and oft-repeated concept of "property tax relief" that they told Republicans who wanted to provide bipartisan cover that they weren't needed.

They were wrong. The 1991 legislative elections resulted in massive Republican victories as taxpayers from Bellmawr to Ewing to Toms River, Woodbridge and Lyndhurst ousted Democratic legislators who supported these taxes. The victory was so complete that Democrats held the Senate and both Assembly seats in only 9 of 40 districts. Republicans held a 58-22 lead in the Assembly, and 27-13 in the Senate – veto-proof margins that allowed Republicans to completely shape the agenda without interference from the electorally repudiated Florio.

Taxpayers put Republicans in charge with a simple message: cut taxes and spending now. The new legislature elected in 1992 took charge by slicing $1 billion from Governor Florio's $15 billion budget request. (Remember we were talking about $6 billion only ten years earlier!) They used this money to roll back the Florio Sales Tax hike and set the rate back to 6 percent. Give us complete control of Trenton and we will do even more, they promised.

But after an initial burst of good policies, Republicans failed. Under pressure from liberal newspapers and interest groups, Republicans under newly elected Governor Whitman scaled back tax cuts for middle-income families earning over $70,000 a year. They moved to take low-income people off the tax rolls, and rejected index-ing tax brackets to inflation, which would prevent people from being boosted into higher brackets due to a rise in the cost of living.

Revenue from hundreds of thousands of taxpay-ers working their way into higher tax brackets, even if the rates in those brackets were reduced slightly, led to massive increases in tax revenues, which generated not additional tax cuts, but an orgy of spending that an un-stable tax source like the income tax could never sustain. Desperate for cash, the state would have to resort to cre-ative borrowing.

State borrowing grew and expanded after Gover-nor Whitman narrowly won re-election in 1997. Within four years, state debt had ballooned to $20 billion with no end in sight. Even so, taxpayers would not see the full impact because the bills for the out-of-control spending were passed off to future generations.

Under Democrats McGreevey, Codey, and Cor-zine, this insane cycle has become even worse. Governor McGreevey, with Codey's support, raised income taxes to 9 percent on "millionaire" families earning over $500,000 a year. The politicians – both Republican and Democrat – who supported this tax hike couldn't spend the money fast enough.

Spending zoomed from $23 billion in the last Whit-man budget to $33.5 billion in 2007 – in just six years. But the new 9 percent income tax actually produced nega-tive revenue, raising $150 million in new revenue with the higher rates that was offset by $250 million lost due to 57,000 high-income taxpayers leaving New Jersey.

Nearly three years ago, I challenged Governor Jim McGreevey on this exact subject at a meeting of Mayors sponsored by the League of Municipalities, which was pushing the McGreevey income tax hike. I was surprised to be recognized when the Governor was seeking comments and told him that this tax money would be spent in a year and the result would be no tax relief and further exodus of "Golden Geese" from our state. Others in the room applauded these comments but legislators, including a number of allegedly "fiscally conservative" Republicans, were unfazed and passed the new 9 percent "millionaire tax," giving Democrats cover for their latest tax scheme.

Two years later, Governor McGreevey's "tax rebates" were eliminated for "rich" taxpayers earning over $100,000 a year and the additional revenue disappeared into the state budget. Our weak and pathetic Republican Party was unable to gain political advantage from any of this because Republicans helped pass these taxes; the result, Republicans, who held 58 Assembly seats after the anti-Florio 1991 elections, were down to just 30 seats. In the Senate they had fallen from 27 to 18. Republicans had sunk to their weakest point since the post-Watergate era.

As bad as things were in the past, however, the current crop of Democrats has made fleecing taxpayers an art form with their new taxes totaling an average additional $8,000 for a family of four from 2001-2006 – and that doesn't count Corzine's restoration of the Florio 7 percent sales tax rate.

And they are not finished yet!

With another false promise to cut property taxes Democrats propose even higher taxes as the solution, combined with what they call "consolidation," which is in reality an effort to eliminate home rule in New Jersey.

Proposals, including some advanced by certain Republicans, call for New Jersey's unique small towns and boroughs to be forced to consolidate into "megacities" and countywide school districts. They refuse to consider any substantial cuts in state employees or cuts in the lavish health, dental, and pension benefits state workers receive. Instead, these Trenton insiders blame local government, never themselves, for the tax crisis our state is in today.

If they are successful, Corzine and his Democratic leadership would place West Milford in the same school district as Paterson and Passaic. They would put Secaucus in the same school district with Jersey City, Runnemede with Camden, and combine Livingston with East Orange and Newark. Hammonton would share a school district with Atlantic City, while Clark would share a school district with Plainfield and Elizabeth.

The result of this so-called "consolidation" is the loss of local citizens' control of local government, local zoning, and neighborhood schools.

Suburban taxpayers would be forced, even more than they are today, to subsidize urban schools and, in fact, proponents are already proclaiming that county-wide school districts would ease the ability to bus children for integration purposes.

This would please the liberals who see our our neighborhoods, taxpayers, and our children as guinea pigs to be experimented on and controlled in social engineering laboratories. However, the actual effect would be to wreck property values, increase the exodus of working families and wealthy people, and turn New Jersey into a state populated predominantly with state employees and welfare recipients, whom history is proving are often the same thing.

High taxes aren't caused by small towns or local zoning or one-family houses on one-acre lots or some town vendor buying a $500 ticket to a political fundraiser. The cause of high taxes is big spending, and until spending is controlled, taxes won't be controlled. It's that simple.

Chapter Four

Education as a Path to Socialism

"When school children start paying union dues, that's when I'll start representing the interests of school children."
--Albert Schanker, President, American Federation of Teachers

The driving force behind spiraling upward taxes in the state of New Jersey has been the cost of education. The push toward centralization, bureaucratization, and governmentalization has taken control of our children's learning out of the hands of parents and teachers and put this sacred responsibility in the hands of liberal elitist bureaucrats.

Today's system of education has evolved from a community-based network of school systems catering to the values, priorities, and vision of parents and their children into an arrogant, centralized bureaucracy that usurps complete authority over what our children will be taught and even tries to dictate what they will be allowed to believe. This is a far cry from the free-thinking, diverse and dynamic education system that made New Jersey an economic powerhouse and source of genius that helped lead our nation.

The history of education's development in this state is one of independent initiative and thinking. Supporters of central government planning constantly pontificate against the many small, independent communities that make up this state. Bent on taking control of all phases of education, the collectivists despise the many small school districts as they are the largest obstacle to completely centralizing control of education.

Independent thought is anathema to centralized thinking. The pioneers, settlers, and immigrants (old and new) that forged New Jersey from wilderness into an economic dynamo and source of tremendous innovation in a relatively short period of time knew the danger of centralized, one-size-fits-all education. That's why so many small towns and school systems exist.

In the nineteenth century, hundreds of small towns and school districts sprang up all over the state. Citizens of New Jersey held the education of their children in high priority and they were willing to do whatever it took to protect their interest. My town of Bogota was a perfect example of the spunky spirit and hard work ethic that dominated the state.

In 1894 the residents of the half-square-mile piece of land that would become Bogota did not want their children traveling to Hackensack to be educated. Primarily Dutch settlers, they wanted to educate their children in their values and ensure their children the individual attention that could only be found in a neighborhood school.

Bogota was chartered and one year later its residents funded and built the borough's first school building. There was no such thing as "state aid." They raised the money through local property taxes, organized a school, and launched a school district that would grow and prosper. The four-classroom school house still serves today as the borough's municipal building.

It's amazing to realize that during a time America was still finding its way as a world power and life was rugged, citizens all over New Jersey had the spirit and determination to commit the resources and make the sacrifices necessary to assure a good education for their children, not forfeit that responsibility to state bureaucrats.

As our nation emerged, Americans were proud to build their communities through volunteerism and hard work. School buildings sprang up as if from the ground all over New Jersey, each funded through local property taxes. From Paterson to Cape May area residents met the need. New Jersey's public education thrived and flourished for over one hundred years alongside and in healthy competition with a robust parochial school system.

Education was affordable and considered a routine part of a community's responsibility. Through WWI, WWII, and the Great Depression, parents, teachers, and local school boards provided one of the finest education systems in the world. As communities and schools grew, more bureaucracy was needed to manage the increase, but out of the healthy need for better control grew the insidious tendrils of centralized thinking, leading to intrusive control of curriculum and mandates that hijacked the control of parents and teachers.

With that centralized bureaucratic control New Jerseyans witnessed the relinquishing of our children's education, and consequently their minds, to Trenton educrats masquerading as experts. Armed with standardized tests these educrats distanced parents and local school boards from any meaningful role in their children's education.

The shift from local and parental control began gradually and has gained momentum over the last forty years.

In the late 1950s the American Federation of Teachers and a small organization called the NJEA Teachers' Union began a public relations campaign geared at passing a broad-based state tax. Even farmers in south Jersey were told they would benefit from abandoning public education funding through property taxes.

The teachers' union's effort continued until their first major victory in 1966 with the passage of the state sales tax. "Better Education through Taxation" was the slogan of the day and the passage of that first broad-based state tax began the shift to centralization of education in Trenton, which inevitably resulted in the gradual loss of parental control.

With the rising cost of education, and the high taxes that are the natural consequence, has come an ever-increasing volume of education lawsuits all serving to move the state's education further into the hands of a centralized bureaucracy. From the framing of the state's constitution in 1875 until only a few years after the passage of the 1966 sales tax, New Jersey's education system ran effectively free of litigation and court-ordered state mandates.

In 1960 Newark was home to Weequahic High School, one of the top-ranked public high schools not just in the state, but in the nation. Newark's public schools throughout the city were well-respected, but the pressure to centralize education opened a floodgate of costly and destructive litigation.

Figure 1 - State Takeover of Education System

Date	Event
Jan 1875	"Thorough and efficient education" Clause established in the New Jersey Constitution
Apr 1966	"Temporary" 3% sales tax adopted as a direct result of the lobbying done by the Teachers' Union
Jan 1967	The NJEA expands and organizes when the American Federation of Teachers pulls out of NJ. It will soon be the most powerful political cartel in the state
Feb 1970	*Robinson v. Cahill*, the first in a series of lawsuits brought by liberal extremists to take control of education away from parents and school boards was decided
Mar 1970	Temporary 3% sales tax is made permanent and raised to 5%, backed by the NJEA
Apr 1973	NJ Court rules that reliance on property taxes for education discriminates against poor districts
Jul 1975	The Public School Education Act creates a new state-funding formula for public schools mandating that state taxes will have to be raised
Jul 1976	Activist Supreme Court closes the public schools for eight days because the Legislature failed to fund the new formula. Governor does not have the guts to stand up to the black-robed oligarchs
Jun 1977	NJ income tax is passed to fund education and provide property tax relief
Feb 1981	Education Law Center (ELC) files infamous *Abbott v. Burke* lawsuit
Jan 1983	2.5 % income tax increased to 3.5%
Jan 1983	Sales tax is increased to 6%, no property tax relief in sight
Jan 1985	NJ Activist Supreme Court issues *Abbott v. Burke I*, remanding control of education to the educrats in Trenton. Governor and Legislators roll over and play dead
1986-87	Trial on Abbott takes place over a 9-month period before Justice Steven LeFelt

Aug 1988	Justice issues a decision that takes control from parents and puts it into the hands of educrats in Trenton. This collectivist maneuver guarantees higher property taxes for suburban homeowners
Feb 1989	Education Commissioner rejects Justice's decision, claims existing funding system works
Jun 1990	Governor Florio passes $2.8 billion tax hike, a major blow to suburban tax payers including new 7% income tax rate
Jul 1990	Extremist NJ Supreme Court decides *Abbott v. Burke II*, devastating the state's public education system and guaranteeing tax increases. This is all part of the collectivist movement
Jul 1994	ELC reactivates the Abbott case charging that the Quality Education Act fails and is not extreme enough
Feb 1995	Extremist Supreme Court declares the Quality Education Act unconstitutional because it is not extreme enough in it's redistribution of suburban tax money to Abbott school systems
Nov 1995	In a bizarre effort to dumb down suburban education, the NJ Department of Education (DOE) releases a blueprint to regulate suburban parents' investment into their children's education
Dec 1996	Governor Whitman unveils a plan to change the school funding formula by capping spending in suburban districts at a minimum level by directing implementation of the Core Curriculum Content Standards
Jan 1997	Governor Whitman signs the Comprehensive Education Improvement and Financing Act (CEIFA) incorporating her plan, without the spending caps in suburban districts. This move gives control to Trenton educrats
May 1997	ELC returns to court to challenge the failure of CEIFA to comply with the 1990 and 1994 Abbott rulings.
Sep 1997	Supreme Court, in *Abbott IV*, declares CEIFA not extreme enough, ordering state officials to immediately increase funding for urban schools
Jan 1998	State redistributes $246 million of suburban tax dollars to corrupt Abbott Districts to comply with extremist court ruling

May 1998	Legislating from the bench is elevated to a new height. Justice orders funding of new programs, including pre-school, at an additional cost of $312 million a year and a program to renovate or replace urban schools
Jul 1999	Supreme Court issues *Abbott V*, ordering radical new programs. Whole school reform, full-day kindergarten and preschool, and major urban school construction all paid for by suburban taxpayers. Social engineering experiments such as school-to-work, after school, and summer school programs expand the nanny state
Mar 2000	ELC returns to Court to force taxpayer funded preschool programs in the Abbott Districts
May 2000	Court forces taxpayers to fund pre K programs in Abbott Districts. This expands ranks of NJEA
Jul 2000	NJ Supreme Court, in *Abbott VII*, orders taxpayers to fund the Abbott Schools Construction program
Apr 2001	Legislature capitulates to activist court and bonds $8.1 billion dollars for school construction statewide
Sep 2001	Justice rules the state failed to properly implement Abbott preschool program ordered in *Abbott V* and *VI*
Oct 2001	NJ Supreme Court hears argument on state's continuing failure to implement preschool
Oct 2001	Appellate Court hears arguments on the failure of the State to establish mandates for local school and district implementation of Abbott programs
Jan 2002	Court demands increased taxpayer funded preschool programs, expanding the state government education system even further
Feb 2002	New $500 S-Corporation Tax aimed at small business
Feb 2002	Supreme Court expands pre-K funding even further
Jul 2002	Governor Executive Order 6 creates massive education bureaucracies
Mar 2003	Governor McGreevey's Executive Order 24 creates the Schools Construction Corp., soon to waste billions of taxpayer $
Apr 2003	Governor McGreevey applies to the Court to remove the mandates for whole school reform and supplemental programs

Aug 2003	Supreme Court directs the DOE to fund the districts at amounts sufficient to maintain expenditures authorized in the 2002-03 budgets
Jan 2004	Bureaucracy ordered in *Abbott X* conjures up complex new mandates and results in the DOE accepting a few and ignoring others
Jan 2004	Governor McGreevey raises income tax to 8.97%. Fourth highest in the nation
Jan 2004	Supreme Court hears appeals by 21 districts challenging the state's failure to provide $150 mil in disputed state aid
Feb 2004	Another bureaucracy established to funnel more suburban tax dollars to Abbott middle and high schools
Jun 2004	Central government educrats begin meeting to develop excuses for failure of massive funding to provide results in Abbott Districts
May 2005	Governor McGreevey signs a bill designating the Salem City public schools as the 31st Abbott District
May 2005	DOE Commissioner launches the Abbott Secondary Education Initiative pouring more tax dollars into Abbott middle and high schools
Aug 2005	Supreme Court orders state to fully fund preschool programs for three and four year olds in Abbott Districts
Jan 2006	Commissioner Librera launches ANOTHER Abbott Secondary Education Initiative, an ambitious program of middle and high school reform in Abbott Districts
May 2006	The NJ State Board of Education rules that students in 16 rural districts, like their urban counterparts, are not receiving a thorough and efficient education under CEIFA
May 2006	Supreme Court allows a one-year Abbott funding freeze, while ordering the State to work with districts to protect wasteful programs, preserving districts' ability to appeal "insufficient State funding decisions"
Jul 2006	A confused Supreme Court appears to reverse its Abbott fund freeze ordering the state to pay all expenses for new and renovated Abbott school facilities opening in 2007

Jul 2007	Sales tax is increased again to 7% equal to the highest in the country

The series of costly lawsuits, funded by the growing leviathan of a state government fed by skyrocketing taxes, continues unmitigated, becoming more abundant and complex with the growth of Trenton's bureaucracy. Control of education has been taken from local school boards and even further out of the hands of parents. As activist justices and education bureaucrats pile on, the state's education system has become a maze of court-ordered mandates.

Government Schools to Expand 20 Percent

As taxpayers brace themselves for more tax increases resulting from government growth, the Corzine administration and the teachers' union bosses at the beck and call of the New Jersey Education Association are planning the largest expansion of the state's public school system in the last one-hundred fifty years.

New Jersey's public school bureaucracy has been quietly taking over the pre-K industry starting in the Abbott Districts. An examination of Governor Corzine's Transition Team Report on education dated January 10, 2006, reveals a call for lifting local school spending limits so every school district can expand into pre-K programs. Corzine himself advocates for what is now called "universal pre-K." Success in this effort would result in massive growth of school budgets and a 20 percent increase in the ranks of the teacher's union, already the most powerful force in New Jersey politics.

The origins of this takeover of private nursery schools can be traced to Governor Whitman's 1995 State of the State Address when she proposed preschools and full-day kindergarten in the special needs districts.

She further pushed her plan on the Gabe Press-
man show in July 2000 when she said, "Preschool for our
children – we have guaranteed that for all our kids in
the state of New Jersey. We are moving rapidly toward
that. And the school construction bill actually will help
in building classrooms for early childhood education."

Considering there are over 200,000 children of
pre-K school age in New Jersey, and at an average cost
of $12,000 per student in the Abbott Districts, the cost to
taxpayers for such a program statewide would be $2.4
billion each year.

The costs of adding so many teachers will have
heavy consequences. When these nursery school instructors retire, a huge new crop of retired teachers will be
piled onto the already teetering system of taxpayer-funded retirement benefits. Yet we're told not to worry about
a thing; the next generation will be stuck with that problem.

Governor Whitman empowered the liberal education activists to push this costly agenda. A plan was
launched to provide pre-K programs for all the Abbott
Districts, but some level-headed individuals argued this
was a violation of the New Jersey Constitution, now a
meaningless piece of paper, which asserts the state must
provide education for children from five to eighteen years
old.

Instead, the state Supreme Court would determine, in its typical convoluted manner, that to provide
education at five years old it was necessary to begin at
three. Egads, why didn't we think of that two hundred
years ago? Carrying out their logic, the next step will be
to begin government-funded education from birth. After
all, aren't those infant years the most formative?

On May 6, 1998, the Supreme Court ordered the
state's taxpayers to "fully fund" pre-K programs in all
Abbott Districts.

From Hoboken to Camden, Abbott District residents could expect to have suburban taxpayers pay for their kids' nursery school tuition, even though suburban taxpayers were experiencing double-digit property tax increases. All the while the state legislature was reduced to a meaningless collection of ineffective elected officials powerless to stop this assault on taxpayers.

Or were they? The consistent pattern that has emerged over the last several decades is the use of the state Supreme Court as an excuse for the growth of government and the implementation of a wide range of new social experiments.

Legislators have had the opportunity – and still do – to introduce a constitutional amendment restricting school funding to its original, practical limits. With the Trenton education bureaucracy and the powerful NJEA teachers' union staring them down legislators did not have the courage to take a stand – even more so with the administration of a "moderate" Republican governor leading the charge.

With government-funded pre-K programs firmly established in the Abbott Districts the Corzine Administration has been positioned to take the next major step. Extra funding from the Schools Construction Corp. had already encouraged suburban school districts to over-build school facilities for future accommodations for pre-K programs. It did not take long for them to make their move.

In my own town of Bogota the Democratic-dominated school board launched its own pre-K program, charging for the 2007 - 2008 school year, $247 per week for a one-half day program. Although government pre-K was paying union salaries and benefits, they were able to beat out the local private nursery school's price of $335 for the same program.

This amounts to nothing more than predatory

pricing practices subsidized with taxpayer dollars. The slow-but-steady expansion of the government school system is happening all over the state and will have devastating consequences for taxpayers, communities, and families.

The free market has responded efficiently and quickly to growing demand for nursery school and after-school services. There are many churches and synagogues that have successfully competed with the private sector in meeting the market demand for affordable nursery schools. These programs have provided revenue helping to keep these non-profit institutions vibrant while meeting the needs of the community.

Strong churches and synagogues uplift a community in other ways, providing a wide range of charitable services and many will be sorely hurt when the government takes over the entire nursery school market. That is the goal of the education bureaucracy and they will stop at nothing to achieve their ends.

A February 2006 report by the National Economic Development and Law Center reported the child care industry is the fastest-growing business sector in the state, with 65,300 full-time jobs, ranking third in employment behind the restaurant and insurance industries, and taking in revenue of $2.55 billion, again ranking third only behind the entire nursing and manufacturing industries. The union bosses recognize this and have leveled their sights on the entire industry.

Over the last ten years the NJEA has made every school employee a member of the union, from lunch room attendants to secretaries and janitors, thereby swelling their ranks and creating more paychecks from which to harvest union dues – a large portion of which are dedicated to political campaigns. This hostile takeover of the nursery school industry will add thousands of new names to the union membership rolls.

The picture is even starker when one reads reports of recommendations submitted to the Child Care Council by William Rodgers, head "economist" of the John J. Heldrich Center for Workforce Development at Rutgers University, calling for an increase in average salaries of nursery school instructors from $29,200 to $47,730, the average salary of an "education worker," as well as the addition of taxpayer-funded union benefits. Rodgers said the child care industry's low visibility is one reason for the low salaries. The state labor department data shows the average wage for preschool teachers in 2004 was $29,200, half the $47,730 average for all education workers.

Rodgers then notes that salaries must be increased to improve the quality of daycare. Dr. Rodgers seems to have little regard for the power of the free market to respond to consumer demand. It is hard to justify labeling the third-largest business sector in the state as having "low visibility," a title that has no meaning.

Rodgers indicates that services will improve simply by increasing salaries, but he does not explain if this requires replacing current pre-K instructors working for these salaries because they are failing to produce at his standard or if simply raising salaries to union standards will equate to improved performance. Rodgers' argument ignores the success of the many parochial schools that have continuously provided quality education while paying salaries far below those in the public-school system.

Taxpayers should be alarmed when an economist employed by the state-run Rutgers University locks arms with the NJEA as part of what is an orchestrated effort to governmentalize the fastest-growing business sector in the state, especially when the expanded programs are at taxpayer expense. The impact of the massive costs associated with this expansion of government will be devastating to property taxpayers.

When the bill hits home, Trenton politicians will call for higher state taxes to end the "property tax crisis" they have caused. Some wide-eyed, "angry" Democrat or "moderate" Republican will jump in front of the television cameras to call for local school districts to be merged because they are inefficient. They will stand in front of an even larger crowd of union-organized protestors in front of the State House to pound their chests and call for "reform" of the "unfair "system of paying for education, all the while ignoring the damage they have created.

The Record wrote about the state's ability to "efficiently" deliver pre-K service versus the free market:

Preschool Accused of Stealing State Funds from Kids

A state grand jury has indicted three leaders of a defunct preschool for needy children for allegedly diverting more than $200,000 in state funds for their personal use. The nine-count indictment against the New Africa Day Care Center alleges that the director, her son and her ex-husband used taxpayer dollars to buy, among other things, two Jaguars and vacations in Chicago and Hyannis Port.

New Africa received about $1.8 million in public funds from January 2001 to March 2004. New Africa was one of hundreds of private centers that signed contracts with the state to provide preschool education for poor 3- and 4-year olds.

Taxpayers have spent $2.5 billion on the so-called Abbott preschool program since it was mandated by the state Supreme Court in 1999.

In April, in a four-part investigative series

called "Lessons in Waste," *The Record* detailed problems in the landmark program, including sloppy bookkeeping at virtually every school, so bad in most cases that auditors couldn't tell how much in state tax money had been spent. The series also noted the state's failure to act against those who allegedly cheated the system.
- *The Record* of Hackensack, June 15, 2006

The Private Sector Solution

The state legislature has been impotent in its ability or willingness to take control of the situation. Governors as far back as Cahill forfeited their leadership to an activist Supreme Court that has regulated and legislated from the bench with nauseating frequency. Any trace of the spunky and spirited drive that was the hallmark of the people of New Jersey has been eradicated in favor of government intervention; all to the detriment of taxpayers and worst of all to the detriment of the children. Our state's public education has become a mediocre diploma mill with 25 percent of high school students graduating with Special Review Assessment (S.R.A.) diplomas.

The NJEA would have citizens believe everything is great. They run commercials telling New Jersey taxpayers how wonderful the public education system is performing, but the public relations rhetoric is far from the truth. Today the United States ranks 30th in the world in math proficiency: New Jersey, once a national leader in education with its neighborhood schools, today ranks high in that mediocrity. This is not good enough for our state; it is time to break the hold of Trenton's bureaucrats and liberal, activist justices. Education should be about children and their parents, not about bureaucrats and union bosses.

Parents and communities must take back control

or risk continuing the dumbing-down of our educational system and our children's minds. To achieve this victory the first step is to take control of the money and give control of education back to parents.

School vouchers put the power to educate in the hands of parents and drive competition. The government school system has a monopoly on education and consumers never benefit from a monopoly. Breaking the hold of this monopoly and forcing free-market competition will return quality results and value driven output to the education system in our state.

In 2005 New Jersey collected $9.5 billion in income taxes. More than 59 percent of that money went to less than 22 percent of the state's students. Those are the pupils in the state's Abbott Districts where spending is averaging over $20,000 per student, well above the per-student average in the suburban districts. Twelve years after the first Abbott decision forced the state to divert almost $38 billion into these districts, Abbott schools still have less than 40 percent of their graduates pass the High School Proficiency Test. The state-mandated system hasn't worked and children are suffering as a result.

Bringing real change, implementing a real solution requires taking on an entrenched establishment that has placed its self interest ahead of our children's future. That entrenched powerhouse is the NJEA teachers' union. Until parents succeed at wrestling control from this political cartel we will not be able to solve the tax problem or make our education system equal to the best in the world; we should settle for nothing less.

The first step is to distribute the state's income tax revenue evenly on a per student basis. This means every community receives the same funding from the state regardless of income, minority breakdown, or any other factor. I cringe at any use of the word "distribute" when it comes to money collected by the state, but the income tax is here for now and can only be reduced as we stabilize spending, which a comprehensive school voucher system can do.

If any school system cannot provide a quality education with these funds supplemented by local property taxes, the parents would receive a voucher for the children to attend the private school of their choice. It is inevitable that the competition forced by such a program will bring change. Many low-income and middle-income families will be able to send their kids to private schools they otherwise could not afford.

Competition would force the public schools to improve in every category from physical plant to curriculum offerings. New and innovative private schools would be opened and bring the economic vitality such institutions provide to neighborhoods. Competition has always forced improvement and benefited the consumer. There is no reason to believe it would not occur in New Jersey's education market. Teachers' union representatives will say we are putting a gun to the heads of teachers, but the unions have been putting a gun to the heads of parents saying, "Here is your school and you will settle for what we offer."

Distributing the state's income tax revenue fairly would cut suburban property taxes an average of 20 percent. School vouchers would drive competition, give parents control of their children's education, and help re-establish New Jersey as a true world leader in education and the resulting prosperity. Re-opening private schools and rebuilding neighborhoods in our beleaguered urban cities, and increasing education productivity to the highest level are byproducts of this kind of dynamic change. So what stands in the way of incredible progress on all these fronts?

As I said before, continuing to follow the same formula for failure is the definition of insanity. New Jersey needs people and politicians to rise up with the courage to take on the entrenched special interests and put taxpayers and children first.

Chapter Five

Mount Laurel Scam

"The belief in the power of free markets is sweeping the world. Eventually it will reach even north Jersey."
--Paul Mulshine, Star-Ledger

Spring 1975 saw the liberal activist New Jersey Supreme Court hand down a shocking decision in what has come to be known as the infamous Mount Laurel Doctrine. The decision was the culmination of a lawsuit filed by a group of "low-income" persons, the kind of low income folks that have the time and money to take a lawsuit to the state Supreme Court. It was filed against the Burlington County community of Mount Laurel and claimed that the town's zoning ordinances discriminated against low-income individuals, thus excluding them from the community in violation of the state's constitutional requirement to "promote the general welfare."

The first *Mount Laurel* decision, *Southern Burlington County N.A.A.C.P. v. Township of Mount Laurel*, 67 N.J. 151 (1975), attacked the system of land-use regulations adopted by the taxpayers in the Township of Mount Lau-

rel on the grounds that low- and moderate-income families were "unlawfully" excluded from the municipality.

In the decision, the Supreme Court held that zoning ordinances that did not provide for low-income,
high-density housing were unconstitutional. This case
is known as *Mount Laurel I* to distinguish it from subsequent litigation.

In *Mount Laurel I*, the Court set forth ridiculous
and draconian mandates for implementing the doctrine.
However, the application of these mandates to particular cases was complex and convoluted, as is typical with
misguided social experiments, so the resolution of many
questions were left uncertain and therefore in the hands
of government bureaucrats. Was the location in question
a "developing municipality?" What was the "region"
and how was it to be determined? How was the "fair
share" to be calculated within that region?

Other questions were similarly troublesome.
When should a court order the granting of a building
permit (i.e., a builder's remedy) to a plaintiff-developer
who has successfully hammered taxpayers by challenging a zoning ordinance on Mount Laurel grounds? How
should courts deal with the complicated procedural aspects of Mount Laurel litigation, such as the appointment
of experts and masters, the joinder of defendant municipalities, and the problem of interlocutory appeals?

The stage was set for Trenton's central government
to intrude into local communities and to force taxpayers
into costly lawsuits to defend their communities from
over-development destined to drive up property taxes
and ruin neighborhoods.

The twisted *Mount Laurel I* decision stunned the
building industry and government officials across the
nation. The justices and low-income-housing advocates
would cheer this destructive decision and claim that
New Jersey had become the leader in "progressive" gov-

ernment housing planning. They indeed revolutionized housing as a function of government. Unfortunately, the revolution more closely resembled the Soviet Revolution than the American Revolution.

The *Mount Laurel Decision*, this doctrine of collectivism and governmentalism, flew in the face of the great values that built this state. For almost two-hundred years, at the time of the *Mount Laurel Decision*, New Jersey had been a place where Americans would come to forge a future, often starting with little or nothing. The early settlers had carved farms and villages out of wilderness.

With the industrial revolution, thousands of Americans flocked to New Jersey to build cities and communities, adapting to the needs of their residents through the free market. Farms, single-family homes on tree-lined suburban streets, apartment buildings in cities like Paterson, row houses in Jersey City, and trailer parks in Lodi met the needs of New Jersey residents.

In my town of Bogota, in the early part of the last century, an adventurous New Yorker willing to settle in the new suburbs could get free architect plans from the New York railroad for a three or four bedroom home if he bought a lot in Bogota. In 1906, an industrious homebuyer could purchase a prefabricated home from a Sears catalog for $1,000 and assemble it themselves. At that time a Tiffany lamp was selling for $750. This is the conservative spirit of independence, personal responsibility, and hard-work ethic New Jersey was made of. Anyone who was "poor" could and would roll up their sleeves and go to work, not whine in front of a judge that they were being discriminated against.

The hard-working immigrants that came to this country understood they had something they could find nowhere else – opportunity. This wealth of opportunity is being eroded away by judicial activism, high taxes, over-regulation, and liberal government policies that replace industriousness with dependence.

Americans take great pride from a history of hard-work and self-reliance. That is our heritage, our culture. My grandparents, on my mother's side, emigrated from Palermo, Sicily, in 1921. My grandfather, Salvatore Trapani, was 17 when he arrived at Ellis Island, sponsored by an uncle and leaving behind his mother, father, and ten brothers and sisters. He had no money and, as he would tell me many years later, was full of hopes and dreams – and scared to death. My grandmother Providenza Pirano arrived with her parents three years later. They found a home in a cold-water flat in Harlem.

Sal and Jenny, my grandmother's nickname, found work in New York City's garment district, Sal as a pattern cutter and Jenny a seamstress. They met on the stoop of that cold-water flat in Harlem and the rest is history. It would be ten years of hard work and saving before these Italian immigrants would save enough money to buy their own home – a small, three-bedroom, one-bath colonial in Ridgefield Park.

When my grandparents came here, there was no Social Security, Medicare, unemployment insurance, or government-funded housing. They didn't expect a hand-out from anyone. When my grandfather brought my grandmother to her new home he carried her across the threshold. They had been married for ten years, but he thought it appropriate and the first thing she did was cry. She was overwhelmed. Only fifteen years after leaving Italy behind with little more than the clothes they carried, they owned a home in the United States of America. They had obtained the American Dream.

This story is not uncommon. Just about every one of us can draw on a background forged from this type of experience. Throughout our nation's history waves of immigrants yearning to be free and willing to work for that freedom have compiled countless stories of commitment to building this nation. All of us can take pride in these tremendous accomplishments, but the Mount Laurel Decision turned that heritage upside down and gutted the very commitment to independence from which Americans have drawn so much strength.

The argument in the *Mount Laurel* case was based on the section of the State Constitution calling for the state to be responsible for "promoting the welfare of its residents." When the framers wrote the constitution "general welfare" referred to protecting freedom, liberty, and the right to the pursuit of happiness as created in our United States Constitution. New Jersey's liberal activist justices twisted this phrase to mean promote the welfare state.

Far from its original intent, the decision broadened this concept to empower the "poor" with a new right, the right to force themselves into a community simply because of their income level. This concept is morally and intellectually bankrupt.

Communities throughout New Jersey establish zoning laws that set forth standards the community chooses to adopt and creates a master plan for future development. In creating and adopting these plans, elected officials conduct a series of public meetings to obtain input from residents and property owners with a vested interest in the community. It is through this process that a community's character is created. Each community has its own personality, and as you would expect, community leaders deal with a variety of disparate challenges and opportunities.

A farm community in Sussex will have far different expectations as to how its town will look compared to a town on Long Beach Island. The needs and wants of homeowners are a major consideration, but so are the needs of businesses, often an important part of the tax base in communities where they are also vital to the area economy.

Homeowners are concerned with maintaining the character and integrity of their neighborhoods and businesses consider conditions like proximity to their market, available workforce, and housing for that work force. Throughout this state's history, local communities have met these challenges successfully. Yes, there are occasional tumultuous run-ins between businesses and residents, but inevitably these issues are resolved and our economy continues to prosper.

Throughout our history, New Jersey towns and villages have met the housing needs of the business sector through the power of that awesome force known as the free market. Now the government of the state of New Jersey, under cover of court orders, has replaced that fair and calibrating ability of the free-market with government force, rendering the plans of local communities impotent in the face of builder's remedies and state-ordered housing quotas.

The fraud of the *Mount Laurel* decision has revealed itself more and more as greater government mandates are set in place through a series of lawsuits designed to justify the government's interference in the housing market.

Within a decade of the original *Mount Laurel* decision, more than one-hundred and forty towns were sued by developers seeking a "builder's remedy." This is a method used by developers to override local zoning ordinances under the pretense that the victim community does not have its fair share of low-income housing.

The builder constructs several low-income units and is then allowed to build many more full-market price units. These below-market price units serve as leverage for builders to develop in areas where they otherwise would not have been allowed.

Since the adoption of *Mount Laurel*, fifteen times

as many full-market units have been built as low-income units. These below-market units have failed to fulfill their original intent because many of these units are occupied by persons of relatively high socioeconomic status who happen to be at the low end of their earning potential, such as graduate students or newly hired NJEA teachers and other government employees.

The *Mount Laurel Doctrine* is a stunning example of social engineering gone wrong. Taxpayers have been forced to spend millions of dollars on lawsuits to defend their neighborhoods. The housing units themselves have failed to fill the need they were intended for and the state has built a giant bureaucracy around this judicial manipulation of the free market. *Mount Laurel* is a throwback to a time when activist justices ordered top-down social change. Housing markets are too complex and dynamic for courthouse engineering. Unfortunately, the Corzine Administration does not get it or does not choose to.

The Corzine agenda is to construct 100,000 "affordable" housing units. That's right - one-hundred-thousand, sort of like one-hundred-thousand teachers or one-hundred-thousand cops. Sounds like someone in the Corzine Administration attended the same big-government, social-engineering marketing school as Bill Clinton.

This proposal is breathtaking in its scope and intent. The Corzine policymakers say New Jersey needs these affordable units for economic development. They say we need this housing to assure there are enough affordable homes for our young people leaving college. Oh, yes! Every morning I wake up and look forward to the day my daughters can graduate from college and move into a government-funded housing unit.

These radical collectivists intend to build many of these units with taxpayer dollars, recreating the failed, low-income housing projects of the sixties in your backyard.

The State of New Jersey Housing Policy and Status Report published August 10, 2006, calls for these projects to be spread equally throughout the state. The big lie to be exposed here is the fact that there is no way any logical plan based on economic need for housing for workers can dictate equally distributing workers throughout the state. Working people would have to be located near areas of employment. This plan is a thinly disguised social engineering scheme that makes New Jersey a magnet state for welfare recipients.

In proposing this radical, collectivist welfare program, the Corzine public relations gurus paint a rosy picture of homes for college students embarking on a career and living units for workers for the new businesses that are just busting down the gates to get into New Jersey. But, an examination of the report reveals a very different picture. The clientele to which this housing will be marketed is listed on page 15, as follows:

"7. Expand community integrated housing opportunities with supports for people with special needs

Special Needs populations include a number of groups such as homeless individuals and families; mental health consumers; persons with develop- mental and physical disabilities, victims of domestic violence, veterans with disabilities, persons with AIDS/HIV, exoffenders re-entering communities from correctional facilities, and youth aging out of foster care or leaving the juvenile justice system. People with special needs are often identified as "hard to house", but frequently can achieve housing stability and independence with long-term housing assistance and supportive services."[1]

Oh, yes, the "hard to house." I am going to go out on a limb here and be politically incorrect - that also means illegal aliens. This is not what America is about. We do not need the government building our housing and we must not allow the government to involve itself in our communities and our lives.

This is pure, unadulterated socialism on a scale seen only in the Soviet Union. Even the Swedish socialists have not extended themselves to such a length. This grotesque policy attacks the very fabric of our communities, interferes with the free market and creates an enormous nanny state. Every resident of this state, rich and poor, must stand up and say no to this travesty.

The true agenda of the collectivist planners who influence and ultimately implement these social-engineering policies is often difficult to clarify. Not so in this case, as shown in the excerpt exposing the actual target market for Corzine's affordable housing units. They are intended for "those leaving the state's correctional system," not the "college students" they claimed.

One of the most revealing examples of the liberal left's true philosophy came in a *New York Times* article titled "Hope and Housing" appearing in the New Jersey section on September 17, 2006. There is no footnote on this quote because the author of this socialist manifesto is listed as anonymous, and the *Times* would not tell me the author's name.

I will endeavor to interpret several key passages, starting with the opening paragraph:

"Housing is one of those emotional terms, like

---

1   Department of Community Affairs, Susan Bass Levin, Commissioner, The State of New Jersey Housing Policy and Status Report, August 10, 2006

terrorism and global warming that bring out a weird sort of anxious fatalism in places like New Jersey. Everyone knows that affordable housing is scarcer than ever; that entire counties have become practically off limits to young people, the elderly and the working class. The usual choices are passive acceptance or abject surrender: turning over half of one's gross income to the mortgage or moving to the Dakotas."

This pathetic diatribe is a radical plea for further expansion of the entitlement mentality that has relegated so many poor souls to wallowing in the welfare state. The American Dream of home ownership earned through personal initiative and industriousness has been transformed into the American nightmare, according to this statement. For centuries, Americans from all walks of life built strength and character from working for independence. To declare that facing the challenge of achieving that dream is akin to facing terrorism or global warming are the words of a coward.

"New Jersey alone will need to accommodate an estimated one million newcomers..."

The mentality of big-government central planners is that should such an influx of population occur in New Jersey it is the government's responsibility to see to it that their housing needs are met. These are the same social engineers who decry "sprawl." Their social-engineering scheme is to force the population into high density housing projects and preserve open space (near their limousine liberal supporters) at taxpayers' expense. Should this population explosion materialize, which is unlikely given the current outward population migration and economic decline, it is not the function of the government to supply housing.

The best method to control sprawl is to allow local governments to uphold their zoning ordinances and protect the character of their neighborhoods. The supply and demand leveling power of the free market will orchestrate the efficient meeting of the economic and demographic needs of the state.

> "'High density' is not a dirty word. And neither is 'affordable housing.' Proposals for affordable multifamily housing often run afoul of the not-unreasonable fear that newcomers with children burden the schools and end up costing a community more than they pay in taxes..."

How loud thou dost protest. The social engineers know individuals understand low-income housing projects are damaging to their neighborhoods. They destroyed communities in the Bronx, Newark, and anywhere else the government forced them in the 1960s. Families and children have been the centerpiece of American neighborhoods and must continue to be strengthened.

The image the planners portray of children being feared because they are too expensive comes from the same radicals that support zero population growth and government-funded abortion as a means of birth control. We must return to a time when children were a welcome and even anticipated addition to our communities, not a blight.

> "Smart is better than dumb. Properly conceived and executed, the philosophy of 'smart growth' involves walkable communities, ready access to mass transit, and architecture that is dense and compact but attractively built..."

The opening sentence is clear. The social engineers are "smart" and the rest of us are "dumb." Compact? Architecturally attractive? Dense? Now the social engineers are deciding what is attractive and what size compartment in which the human organisms will be allowed to exist. That is, as long as those human organisms walk and get out of their stupid automobiles, being the environmentally destructive parasites that we are.

"New Jersey seems to be getting the message. High-density projects have been built or are underway adjacent to train stations in places like South Orange, Union Township and Cranford. This is a hopeful sign. If the region is ever going to break its addiction to the car and end the curse of low-density sprawl, communities arranged on smart-growth principles will lead the way."

The message cheered on by those that would have government intrude on the American Dream is being shoved down our throats by court orders obtained by spending millions of taxpayer dollars on lawsuits. The message is simple: collectivist planners are going to force you into high-density housing and out of that comfortable little home with the white picket fence.

"Big government is not the problem. Little government is. Hundreds of local municipalities make decisions about land use, and their individual acts of resistance to housing solutions have left the whole region worse off. State and county governments cannot rely on the bully pulpit alone; they need broad strategies for planning and managing growth. The report describes New Jersey's plan as one of the nation's most comprehensive. The rest of the tri-state region scores lower: Connecticut's plan is purely advisory, and New York's is nonexistent."

The social engineers recognize that those pesky local governments, which Thomas Jefferson declared were the governments closest to the people, are citizens' last line of defense against a master plan for directing their futures. Big-government planners fear that local government will stop the agenda of the nameless, faceless central planners. Remember, the author of this manifesto is "anonymous."

These social engineers describe resistance in the suburbs as like the resistance to the invading Nazi forces that threatened to destroy every country in its path: a curious definition for these invading social engineers to adopt for their opposition.

"We're all in this together. The report concludes by stressing that the region's far-flung suburbs are all extremities of one social and economic organism. It's an integrated body, and solutions in one area will help communities elsewhere. The region is large, sprawling and full of competing interests and rivalries, but affordable housing is the quandary that unites us all."

With apologies to the author, I'm going to be a little politically incorrect; this sounds like pure communism. Pardon my resistance.

To summarize, the social engineers and central planners will preserve open space for deer and rabbits to roam freely while the human population will be shoehorned into high density, compact but attractive (by government standards) housing projects where citizens will be broken of the awful habit of wanting to drive their cars.

Nothing to worry about because each of these model "transit villages" will feature a shiny new government day care center where residents can deposit the children and hop on the taxpayer-subsidized, "environmentally friendly" light rail to head out to their government job (the only sector to be still experiencing job-growth).

But on the way home, citizens should be sure to stop by the government-funded senior housing project to visit mom and dad. This is the life social engineers would have you believe is wonderful: The American Dream, utopia.

Chapter Six

The Myth of Consolidation

"Without power and independence, a town may contain good subjects, but it can have no active citizens."
--Alexis de Tocqueville

The cornerstone of conservative philosophy regarding the operations of government rests on the belief that small government is essential to the protection of our most fundamental rights. The ability of average citizens to have entry to and genuine influence over the management of their community has flourished under the American model of government.

The renowned French writer Alexis de Tocqueville marveled over the effectiveness of small, local governments in New England and their uniquely American character. It was clear to de Tocqueville that these governmental units afford citizens the ability to govern themselves and control their own destinies. Early on, conservatives recognized the importance of local governments in safeguarding against the gradual move toward collectivism and totalitarianism that history shows is the result of centralized power.

The Framers of the Constitution understood the importance of limiting the power of the federal government and safeguarding state rights. Life under the thumb of British imperialism had given them a healthy distrust of government power. The Declaration of Independence contains a litany of governmental abuses, including dissolution of representative Houses, obstruction of the administration of justice, and taxes without consent, just to name a few.

The Framers knew the monarch was not going to just roll over and cede his power to the colonies. Historically, major moves by any oppressed populace toward independence have been grounds for military action. This is why the Declaration of Independence ends with, "and for the Support of this Declaration, with a firm Reliance on the Protection of Divine Providence, we mutually pledge to each other our Lives, our Fortunes, and our sacred Honor."

The iron hand of an oppressive regime is not easily thrown off and has a way of creeping back in as people succumb to the vagaries of power. The Framers knew that on the state level the rights of local towns and villages to self-govern had to be strenuously protected. Local communities that take pride in their identity and value their special characteristics jealously guard their independence.

Perhaps more than most states, New Jersey's towns and villages have historically valued this tradition, and rightfully so. This state has led the nation in economic development for two centuries. New Jersey led the nation in transitioning from an agricultural economy after the Civil War to a manufacturing economy as a result of the Industrial Revolution. The transition took place as a result of local control and local initiatives to maximize geographic and demographic resources.

Paterson used its waterfalls to drive hydroelectric power plants and become the nation's leader in silk manufacturing. Trenton's central riverfront location helped that city expand manufacturing and boast the slogan, "Trenton Makes – The World Takes." Camden's proximity to Philadelphia and a harbor made it the ideal city for manufacture of the famous Victrola and for Joseph Campbell to launch the all-American Campbell's Soup Company.

New Jersey's urban industrial centers were a model for the rest of the country. What makes this transition so remarkable by today's standards of government interference is the fact that it took place with no government subsidies, no over-staffed State Department of Economic Planning, and no governor claiming he/she would be the state's chief marketer, as Governor Jon Corzine announced in 2006.

Far from driving out businesses, the small size of the state government and reliance on local governments made the state an ideal place to set up shop. Free from big government interference and gridlock, local governments could adapt deftly to local needs without fear of bureaucrats and government officials seeking a piece of the action.

It is disturbing to listen to elected officials willing to throw "home rule" (what built this state) under the proverbial bus. These cries for consolidation are cheap sound bites from elected officials with no knowledge of the importance and the effectiveness of local government. Those who spout this nonsense either have no understanding of this issue or simply are willing to sacrifice self-government for political purposes. I don't know which is worse.

The term "home rule" has been coined by the liberal media, which advocates consistently for onerous centralized government. The rights of the individual to self-govern are seen as being at odds with the need of the government to rule with central authority. The term "home rule" is most often treated by the media with contempt since they equate the concept of self-government with selfishness.

This interpretation is rather curious, as the right to rule over one's own home has long been considered sacred. Giving up the right to determine one's destiny is something any healthy person should fight to avoid, which is why the socialists have such a need to create entrenched constituencies for big-government programs - in other words a dependent populace that relies on handouts from Big Brother.

At first blush such big-government welfare programs might appear to be borne from a populist mindset, but in fact these programs characterize an elitist world view. Such programs are created by ultra liberal collectivists who believe from the depths of their patrician cockles that the proverbial unwashed masses are incompetent to govern themselves. And since home rule stands in the way of imposing an elite central authority, steamrolling over it is a key goal of collectivists. Fundamentally eliminating home rule is to indicate that a man's home is not his castle; it is only through the benevolence of the State that his "home" is made possible.

In a May 28, 2006, *New York Times* article by Mitchell Blumenthal entitled "Tough Talk on Home Rule, But is it Just Talk?," Governor Corzine is quoted from his days as a senator, "The immense burden of hundreds of tiny governments is extracting an exorbitant tax."

This statement is intellectually bankrupt for a number of reasons. First, the central state government's budget is spiraling out of control at many times the rate of inflation while state debt is reaching crushing proportions. State spending, not local spending is extracting an exorbitant tax burden from our taxpayers.

Second, the facts prove incontrovertibly that small towns in New Jersey are far more efficient and cheaper to operate than any large city. For example, in 2004 Bogota had a per capita municipal operating expense of $741.[1] Newark, on the other hand, spent a ridiculous $2,039[2] per capita to operate its overfed government apparatus. Worse yet, Newark requires massive amounts of state financial aid to keep its big-government bureaucracy afloat, at the expense of suburban taxpayers in small towns like Bogota.

Despite this obscene level of overspending, Corzine continues to distract voters with misleading sound bites. "Why should we have all these small town mayors and police chiefs?" asks Governor Corzine. The answer to that question is one that Governor Corzine already knows - by weakening local control, big-government and the bureaucracy that comes with it is strengthened. Bureaucracies are the antithesis to running government like an efficient business, as Governor Corzine claims it should be.

The British physician Max Gammon first developed the theory of Bureaucratic Displacement after studying the government-run British health care system. He concluded that "in a bureaucratic system increase in expenditure will be matched by a fall in production." In other words, bureaucratic systems are rife with inefficiencies, sucking resources and shrinking production.

Consider McDonald's Corporation as a business model. It is the largest and most successful fast-food provider in the world and has a separate franchise owner for each store. This is diametrically opposed to the philosophy of centralized government some policymakers hope to force on frustrated New Jersey residents as an answer

---

1   *Star Ledger* Tax Analysis Website: http://www.nj.com/news/ propertytaxes/index.ssf?/str/taxes/rank/../default.asp
2   Ibid

to their concerns regarding skyrocketing property taxes.

Well-run businesses understand the value of decentralized management and the pride of ownership that comes with it. As Mayor of Bogota, I have seen our borough council take an interest in examining and questioning even the smallest bills. Such scrutiny is not occurring in Trenton.

New Jersey residents suffer from the highest property taxes in the nation, our top income tax rate is the fourth highest in the nation; and we have the highest sales taxes. There is no question New Jersey citizens are among the highest taxed in the country. The question is why?

Governor Corzine and his minions would like to turn New Jersey's wide array of small towns and municipalities into scapegoats for the problems their policies have created. In a July 28th article published in *The Record* by Senate Majority Leader Richard Codey, he states "New Jersey currently has 566 municipalities, 616 school districts and 186 fire districts, which along with our 21 counties rely on property taxes to fund their operations." Codey makes this statement as if the numbers of local governing entities alone are sufficient to explain New Jersey's sky high taxes. And unfortunately, many ill-informed politicians are coalescing around the false solution of forcing the merger of municipalities.

The facts do not support this misguided scheme. An analysis of the cost of local government proves the opposite. Smaller municipalities have lower per capita operating costs.

With unchecked growth of bureaucracy, the bigger the town, the more difficult it becomes for Joe Taxpayer to fight City Hall, let alone accomplish necessary government related business. Pity the hapless citizen who tries to get a simple building permit or even a marriage license in Newark.

Figure 2 - Comparison of Small Town Municipal Cost versus Large Cities for Year 2004

Town	Popu-lation	Munici-pal Cost in mil-lions	Per capita cost	Cost per hom-eowner	State Aid per Hom-eowner
Hopewell	2.051	$2.185	$1,066	$3,311	$418
Magnolia	5,326	$4.649	$873	$3,374	$773
Hightstown	5,326	$4.649	$873	$3,374	$773
Bogota	8,208	$6.085	$741	$3,017	$539
Guttenberg	11,011	$12.126	$1,101	$5,314	$465
Haddon-field	11,596	$10.771	$929	$2,652	$352
Cedar Grove	12,565	$10.194	$811	$2,795	$432
Verona	13,315	$14.990	$1,126	$3,106	$360
Fairview	13,561	$11.763	$867	$5,809	$734
Hawthorne	18,378	$15.250	$830	$2,854	$384
West Milford	28,217	$27.166	$963	$2,771	$328
Ewing	37,057	$36.015	$972	$3,501	$1,275
North Bergen	58,004	$61.703	$1,064	$6,228	$941
Camden	79,948	$141.082	$1,765	$6,897	$2,718
Trenton	85,379	$156.822	$1,837	$7,515	$2,549
Jersey City	239,079	$366.174	$1,532	$11,467	$2,551
Newark	280,451	$572.041	$2,040	$21,083	$4,111

It is far easier and more common for taxpayers in small towns to monitor how their tax dollars are spent. A taxpayer in White Township has a much simpler job learning how the governing body is spending his or her money than a taxpayer in Newark or Jersey City. Hence, corruption and waste, which run rampant in large cities, are far less prevalent in small towns.

When it comes to educating the next generation

of New Jerseyans, smaller towns also outperform larger, more bureaucratic systems. The best public school systems in the state are those in small towns, and not because they are better funded. Due to the Abbott decision, schools in Newark, Camden, and other cities receive state funding to bring their per-student spending above what the best small school districts spend.

The reason towns like Ridgewood, Moorestown, and Sparta have such excellent schools is effective parental involvement. Combining school districts would weaken the ability of parents to influence school activities and many parents would be dissuaded from participating when confronted with the bureaucracy of a larger system because dealing with a bloated state school system is much more daunting than a streamlined local one.

Finally, the argument against consolidation is not purely for the sake of home rule. Democracy as we know it cannot survive without a strong dose of local government. Too often we take for granted the marvelous fact that in these communities anyone willing to work hard can be part of government. Surgeons, plumbers, store clerks, engineers, anyone willing to ask their neighbor for their vote can be an elected official and play a role in the governing of their community.

Those leading the left keep forgetting, or more likely ignoring, the fact that local control and governance is part of the system that puts the power of self-government in the hands of the people. If power is in the hands of the people, the government has less, and the liberal elites hate that. Human nature being what it is, local politics can often be rough-and-tumble and sometimes seem tumultuous and unproductive. The end result, however, is that we become a better community and a stronger nation because of the process.

Governor Corzine (and on a national level, his party) would like to wipe out local breeding grounds for democracy. To him, these towns and villages are a nuisance standing in the way of the planned expansion of Trenton's central government.

Hillary Clinton said it takes a village, but what people of her ideology never tell you is, in their view, the village has to be tightly controlled and regulated by a massive central government machine, and they are the only ones smart enough to run it. In Governor Corzine's world, only those liberal elites connected to the political machine, backed by Big Labor or their own millions of dollars would be elected or allowed to govern.

If New Jersey is going to continue to provide government of the people, by the people, and for the people, we citizens must vigilantly protect government at the local level - government that the people can access.

To avoid accountability for their past mistakes and to disguise their lack of principle, many feckless politicians would like us to believe New Jersey's high taxes can be mitigated by empowering the state to force consolidation of small towns. This is yet another desperate attempt to divert attention from the out-of-control spending these politicians have presided over.

Consolidation moves municipalities inexorably toward centralization, and centralization grows government... every time. Contrary to what some lawmakers may say, it is not possible to both grow government and lower taxes, no matter how the facts may be twisted. Once centralized services have been created, they must be administered and that takes money, money, and more money. As for citizens, no one really wants to live in a state that is full of cities run as well as Newark, Trenton, and Camden. The dangers of consolidation and centralization is not a conclusion reached by rocket science, but simple, common sense.

If lawmakers want to cut taxes without creating a deficit, they have to cut spending. If they want to cut spending, they have to shrink government. It simply isn't fair or reasonable to impose high taxes on the rest of the state so that Newark can have pet projects, or to subsidize the marketing of New Jersey raised crops, or for state employees to work 35 hour weeks and retire at 55, and so the taxpayer's tab reaches to the tune of $33 billion per year and rising.

The answer to high taxes lies in more local control, not less.

If the New Jersey Legislature would simply rescind some of the costly mandates imposed on local government - such as requiring all employees be enrolled in the state's outdated pension system - property taxes could be cut.

Governor Corzine likes to claim he will run New Jersey like a business. This is bad news for New Jersey citizens. Government is not and never has been a business. Even if it were, Corzine has no intention of running it like a business, unless by business he means inefficient, over-funded, despotic, financially irresponsible, and designed to strip power from the individual citizen and stuff it into the greedy fingers of liberal bureaucrats.

Please, no more nonsense about running the state like a business. Businesses are expected to maximize profits for executives and shareholders and provide luxurious offices, cars, and perks. This is only appropriate, since business owners have shouldered the risk and pain to gain these rewards. At a high cost to taxpayers, too many in government expect similar rewards without the same level of personal risk.

If we hope to have a nation where power remains in the hands of the people, bigger can never be better. If citizens value their personal freedom, when it comes to government, small is beautiful. Distribution of governmental power through autonomous local governments that citizens can constrain is the best way to protect our individual freedoms. Consolidation is nothing more than a power grab by the liberals in office, no matter what their public or campaign disguise; it must be resisted at every turn.

Chapter Seven

What Did She Do?

"I'll gladly pay you Tuesday for a hamburger today."
--Wimpy

Over the last 10 years New Jersey has experienced an explosion in new debt never before seen in state history. Our debt is the fastest growing debt in the country, elevating New Jersey to third place for having the highest per capita debt in the nation at $3,460 for every man, woman, and child.

At a time when our nation was experiencing remarkable economic growth New Jersey chose to defer its obligations to the next generation, mortgaging the wages of our children and grandchildren yet unborn. Even the World War II generation, following the Great Depression and the remarkable commitment to our freedom to which they had sacrificed themselves, did not incur such a debt.

This is the wreckage left in the wake of a gang of reckless and irresponsible politicians more concerned with their own self-aggrandizement than the future of our state. Worse yet, this debt is the legacy of a generation robbed of the right to vote on actions as profound as reaching into the pockets of their children and fueling the massive growth of big government. This inexcusable usurpation of responsibility comes from the same political automatons that pontificate "home rule" as the problem with our state.

The New Jersey state government is not the answer to the problem of burdensome taxation and debts, it is the problem.

The questions citizens must now answer is who is responsible and how do we get back on track?

Since 1997 the government of New Jersey has borrowed over $16.9 billion to cover budget deficits. This staggering figure is taken from a chart shown on the New Jersey Treasurer's website at www.nj.gov. That $16.9 billion represents money borrowed using long term financing to pay for a massive expansion in state government including thousands of new state (read taxpayer funded) employees and a bevy of new social welfare programs.

During this period of exploding debt the state budget doubled from $16.0 to $33.6 billion today. The growth in broad-based state tax revenues could not keep pace with the credit-card mentality in Trenton that catered to the ravenous appetite of a central bureaucracy that has known no limits to expanding power. To supplement the flow of money, bureaucrats, with lawmakers at their beck and call, had to find and employ every trick and gimmick possible.

The borrowing frenzy started during the Whitman Administration when financial wizards conjured up the scheme of bonding $2.8 billion to shore up the defined-benefit pension system, rather than embrace reform, and fund current expenses.

Through this manipulation the Whitman Administration was able to fund the state's annual appropriation from the proceeds of the bond issue rather than direct taxation to the tune of $500 million, in essence funding a current expense over the next twenty years. The rest of the proceeds were invested in the stock market with the expectation of an annual 10% return over the life of the bonds. The state was playing fast and loose with taxpayer indebtedness by gambling on the market and now the taxpayers have to cover the losses.

Then the largest bond issue in United States history authorized by a state without the approval of its voters was conspired in New Jersey. Using the activist New Jersey Supreme Court to demand the state spend $3.1 billion for school construction (see Chapter 4) the Whitman Administration had the excuse they needed to float the largest debt issue New Jersey had ever seen.

Governor Whitman and the Republican controlled Senate and Assembly then took the runaway debt train down the track to ruin, "flipping the bird" to conservatives who believed in constitutional restraint and sound fiscal management. After months of backroom deal-making between Republicans and Democrats, the legislature schemed to borrow $8.6 billion for "school construction" in urban and suburban districts. Legislators in affluent suburban districts exchanged their sworn oath to uphold the Constitution of the State of New Jersey in favor of the misguided belief that they were "bringing money back" to their districts. Lawmakers violated the Debt Limitation Clause established in the State Constitution in 1875 and reestablished in 1947.

In 1875 the New Jersey Legislature had adopted the Debt Limitation Clause as a defense against reckless borrowing after several states had declared bankruptcy, defaulting on obligations when tax revenue declined due to recession. The clause states:

"The Legislature shall not, in any manner, create in any fiscal year a debt or debts, liability or

> liabilities of the State, which together with any previous debts or liabilities shall exceed at any time one per centum of the total amount appropriated by the general appropriation law for that fiscal year... except as hereinafter provided, no such law shall take effect until it shall have been submitted to the people at a general election and approved by a majority of the legally qualified voters of the State voting thereon."[1]

Decades later the 1947 Constitutional Convention reestablished this important protection. The principle behind the debt limitation protection is that no legislature should have the power to authorize debt that will be foisted on future legislatures. The reason is simple. Members of the New Jersey General Assembly are elected to a two-year term and cannot be allowed to make decisions that cannot be reversed by future Assemblies. These decisions must be decided by the electorate. Constitutional Amendments and debt the state is obligated to repay must therefore be brought before the voters. The concept is sound and for over one-hundred years kept New Jersey's government financially responsible.

There is an underlying premise that supports the reasoning behind this constitutional clause - the voters are smarter than the body of elected officials representing them and will make better decisions about policy issues that will have long-term impact.

This premise includes an automatic assumption that any governing body is capable of being corrupted not just in the criminal but also in the political sense of selling out taxpayers to buy votes. With the rise of the ultra-liberal New Jersey Supreme Court and the increasingly liberal Whitman Administration agenda, for the first time the government and its minions had chosen to

---

1   New Jersey State Constitution, Article VIII Section II

supersede the electorate. No more government by the people – the people are too stupid.

The Framers of the Constitution saw this challenge to the people's authority coming and took every precaution to ensure it did not happen. But to uphold these protections would require a state supreme court willing to enforce the constitution or a state legislature with the backbone to stand up to an activist court that would not fulfill this obligation. New Jersey has neither. The consequences have become apparent.

Few things are as aggravating as an elected body that will not follow through on sworn duties. Since being elected mayor in 1995 I had been committed to reducing Bogota's debt. The Democrats our Republican team defeated on a promise to return fiscal responsibility to Bogota, had gone on a bonding spree borrowing for items as trivial as fax machines and other current expenses. Instead of budgeting wisely, Bogota leaders racked up debt for everyday expenses, the equivalent of a family mortgaging their home to buy lottery tickets.

Now the state government, under control of my own Republican party, was on a borrowing rampage like nothing before in the state's history. Growing up in an Italian immigrant household where saving was the way to build for the future and credit card borrowing was considered nothing short of evil, this new, big-government credit-card policy ran contrary to everything I believed.

It didn't matter if the governor was a Republican; I was not going to tolerate this without a fight. So I did what any other self-respecting conservative activist would do, I called for a meeting at my home of anyone who cared.

More than 40 New Jerseyans gathered at my Bogota home on December 3, 2000 to form Stop the Debt. This was a collection of outstanding individuals from varying backgrounds and of various political beliefs. The turnout was larger than expected. We had sent out emails, made a few calls and expected a handful of citizens - we had standing room only.

The debt issue hit a nerve in a big way. These folks knew racking up massive amounts of debt without so much as a nod in voters' direction was fundamentally wrong. People were ready to act. We passed the hat and raised the money to file one of the most important lawsuits in the state's history to defend New Jersey voters' rights to restrict the growth of state government.

The lawsuit centered on the state's practice of circumventing the Debt Limitation Clause by setting up front groups called "authorities." These bogus entities borrowed money and allowed big-spenders to claim the debt was not really the responsibility of the state and therefore did not require voter approval.

This practice had begun with the New Jersey Turnpike Authority, which bonded money to construct the turnpike but had a real revenue stream of its own from tolls. This concept was the subject of litigation in 1945. The courts recognized the Turnpike had a legitimate income of its own and could repay its debt without funding from the legislature.

The establishment of the Schools Construction Corporation within the Economic Development Authority was quite different. This phony authority had no ability to raise a dime. The only source of income would be from the state budget - the taxpayers of New Jersey. Bonding money to the Economic Development Authority was a sneaky financial trick with the goal of circumventing the state constitution's requirement of voter approval of debt.

The case seemed clear to most except the state Supreme Court which would once again abdicate its responsibility to uphold the constitution. Editorial support ran heavily in favor of my challenge. Even liberal newspapers concluded the courts had to uphold this simple standard and that allowing phony front groups to sink the state into debt and rob the voters of their rights was unacceptable.

Lonegan v. New Jersey took months and tens of thousands of dollars to wind its way to the New Jersey Supreme Court. During this long legal process the State Attorney General issued a directive that any bond issue sold by the state but not approved by the voters must display a disclaimer. This became known as the "Lonegan Disclaimer."

I am proud of that small achievement, but Wall Street did not seem to consider it important and it had little or no impact on the bond sales. Wall Street portfolio managers would do well to consider the subtle message, sometimes called "fine print," which clearly explains that the state has no responsibility should the "authority" granted the loan decide to default.

Hold onto your wallets investors - these "independent authorities" have gone bankrupt before and history has a way of repeating itself.

The landmark case was finally heard by the Supreme Court in July 2000. The court split the case into two parts. While the suit focused on all authority debt issued without voter approval a major component was the School Construction bonds. *Lonegan v. New Jersey 1* dealt with only the School Construction bonds and *Lonegan vs. New Jersey 2* with the practice of issuing all other authority debt without voter approval. The decision in *Lonegan 1* was handed down in August, 2002 and it was no surprise. The court abandoned any principle of constitutional restraint and determined its earlier mandate that more money be spent on school construction was reason enough to override voters' rights.

The court conveniently forgot it had ordered $3.1 billion for school construction, yet the bond issue in question had grown to $8.6 billion as a result of backroom deals. This decision was hard enough to handle, but I felt confident this meant the rights of voters would be upheld to stop other borrowing schemes.

Andrew T. Fede, Esq., argued the case from the beginning. His briefs were scholarly and on-point. It was obvious during the hearings that the Justices respected his arguments. Justice Gary Stein wrote a powerful dissenting opinion in *Lonegan 1*.

The division of the case into two parts, the powerful and articulate dissenting opinion of Justice Gary Stein and the overwhelming editorial support seemed to indicate the court would make the right decision and uphold the constitutional right of voters to approve or deny new debt. However, there was a last minute change.

Chief Justice Deborah Poritz delayed the final hearing for months. This delay tactic lasted long enough for Justice Gary Stein, whose vote in deciding the case would prove to be critical, to retire at the end of September 2002. New Governor Jim McGreevey appointed Justice Barry Albin to the bench and on October 21, 2002 the Supreme Court heard *Lonegan v. New Jersey 2*, Justice Albins's first case. The hearing that day was marked by final oral arguments by Fede for the taxpayers and Alison Accurso for the state. The most telling question of the day came from Justice Albin when he asked my attorney, "If Mr. Lonegan is not happy with the legislature's borrowing practices why doesn't he run a slate of candidates in the next election?" There are 120 senators and assemblymen. It became apparent how Justice Barry Albin felt about constitutional taxpayer protections.

The New Jersey Supreme Court rendered its decision in *Lonegan vs. New Jersey 2* on April 9, 2003. The decision was a devastating 4-3 loss for taxpayers with newly appointed Justice Barry Albin voting with the majority.

This is the most expensive example of judicial activism in our state's history. By striking down the Debt Limitation Clause, the court released the state government on a runaway borrowing spree that has driven our debt to astronomical levels in only a few short years.

There is no better description of the consequences of this decision than the opening sentence of the dissenting minority opinion, "Today's decision construes the Debt Limitation Clause so narrowly that the clause no longer applies, except in those increasingly rare instances when the state seeks to incur general obligation indebtedness."

Only in critically important decisions do all the justices take the time to sign the dissenting opinion. Justices Long, Verniero and Zazzali felt this abuse of power so egregious that they all put their signatures on the dissent.

At the press conference following the Supreme Court's gutting of our constitutional protections, which permitted the governor and legislature to float as many School Construction Bonds as they desired, I warned this project would be the biggest scam the state had ever seen. I forecasted that there would be a lot of newly wealthy contractors and assorted professionals tooling around New Jersey in new BMWs. Indeed, with the awarding of contracts school construction costs skyrocketed.

It did not take long for my predictions to come true even beyond my worst fears. From the beginning, the Schools Construction Corp. was riddled with massive corruption and nothing more than a pot of money wide open to political payoffs and fraud. The corruption was so bad it has made the Schools Construction Corporation (SCC) the poster child for reform and anti-corruption laws.

There are too many cases of taxpayer rip-offs to list, but several of these creative scams merit recognition, such as the $1.7 million dollar renovation of a brand new

Long Branch school. Another example of misused tax dollars was $340,000 for a mailing that had nothing to do with school construction and everything to do with Governor McGreevey's book club. The mailer was printed by a company that had donated $5,000 to McGreevey's gubernatorial campaign. Then there was the spending of $330 million on "environmentally contaminated" land, in other words land that is so toxic and radioactive that schools can never be built on it. The property in question was once the site of the original Manhattan Project in Union City.

Add the blatant waste of $100 million for schools in Trenton and Newark; these were not several schools in each city but two schools at $100 million each. Of course, don't forget the purchasing of clocks for the Paterson Schools, which cost taxpayers $600 each. These are just a few of the blunders that have happened at the hands of the SCC - debacles that have cost New Jersey taxpayers hundreds of millions of dollars.

With the court ruling against taxpayers in *Lonegan 2*, I again forecasted the future with accuracy. I predicted the decision would lead to unlimited borrowing and ultimately the use of debt to fill budget deficits. The constitution was designed to prevent such abuse, but once that pesky document was out of the way the legislature had carte blanche to bond to their hearts content. Lawmakers would take advantage of the opportunity sooner than even conservatives expected.

In 2003 Governor Jim McGreevey turned bonding into a new art form. The state had settled a massive class action law suit against the tobacco industry and was slated to receive payments over 25 years intended to offset the expense of smoking related illness added to Medicaid and state health insurance costs. Enter stage left the financial wizards from the same cult that brought the pension bond scheme. Conveniently forgetting the purpose of the tobacco settlement (which was apparently just courtroom rhetoric), the trick lawmakers played was to leverage the tobacco settlement money for borrowing so they could pay the year's budget deficit and still give out "goodies" in the form of more government jobs.

Conservatives understand the importance of constitutional limitations. When liberals talk about "living constitutions" they have one goal: the same kind of scheming manipulation of our constitutional protections that took place with the New Jersey Supreme Court in this critical case. It is essential to big-government progressives and central planners to remove the barriers to government growth established by the constitution. In 2004 Governor Jim McGreevey and the Democratic-controlled legislature dropped any pretense of following constitutional limits and made a move considered outlandish even by many liberals.

In June 2004 Governor McGreevey was faced with a $2 billion budget deficit if he didn't stop the runaway spending that had driven the state budget up to $25.7 billion from $21.6 billion in just three years. Governor McGreevey and the Democrats had no intention of doing so. They simply pulled out the state's giant credit card and announced they would borrow $2.1 billion to pay current expenses.

What would Republicans do about it? After all, they were the gang that started this nonsense with the pension and school construction bond schemes. Within hours of the announcement, I contacted attorney Fede, now known for his knowledge of state constitutional debt issues throughout the legal profession, and told him it was time to roll into action. "This is over the top," Fede said, "There is no way the court can allow this." Fede was right to be shocked, but this is New Jersey and we have the nation's most liberal activist court.

When Stop the Debt announced the lawsuit in

One Time Tricks and Gimmicks

More Than $16 Billion of One-Time Revenues and Pension
Contribution Deferrals Can Not and Should Not Continue
($ in millions)

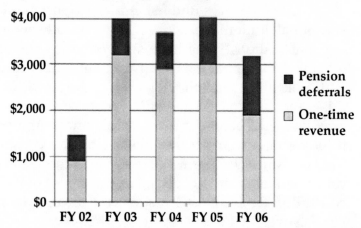

2000 against Republican Governor Whitman and the
Republican-controlled senate and assembly, my fellow
conservative activist supporters and I were alone. I was
told I was persona non grata and had no future in the
Republican Party. Four years later when I called a similar press conference in the Hughes Justice Complex most
of the Republican Party legislators couldn't get there fast
enough. They even tried to push me out of the photo
to the amusement of the press who had been with me
through the earlier efforts.

State Senator and minority leader Leonard Lance
announced he would file on behalf of the legislative minority. As a member of the Assembly until 2002, Senator
Lance had been one of the courageous few who had voted
against the school and pension bond schemes. Senator
Lance told me that he was informed by the Republican
leadership back then that there would be consequences
for his actions. The following year he was passed over
for Chairman of the Assembly Budget and Appropria-

tions Committee.

The suit was joined by Alex DeCroce, Assembly minority leader. The brunt of the work in preparing briefs and arguing the case fell on Fede who was clearly the most experienced and capable, even though I agreed to let Senator Lance be the lead plaintiff in that case. Mark Sheridan Esq., representing DeCroce and Lance, helped strengthen Fede's argument and his assistance proved invaluable in developing our pro-taxpayer argument.

The decision in this case was one of the most bizarre in the annals of even the New Jersey Supreme Court. The justices ruled that bonding for current expenses was unconstitutional and would not be allowed, but Governor McGreevey could get away with it this one time. What's $2.1 billion between friends?

Between 1997 and 2006 the state government borrowed $16.9 billion to cover current expenses and close budget gaps. Governor Jon Corzine displayed this fact with a chart on the www.nj.gov website and used it in his town hall meetings to demonstrate the irresponsible management of past administrations.

The governor's transition team report dated January 10, 2006 calls for an end to "tricks and gimmicks" used to balance the budget. Conservatives have called for just that type of prudent fiscal management for decades.

But the Corzine rhetoric has proven to be just that, rhetoric. In the first nine months of the Corzine administration the state's debt increased $3.3 billion to an all-time high of $33 billion. The Democrats' financial advisors found another way to borrow another huge pot of money. On November 7, 2006 a ballot question was approved by New Jersey voters that promised to dedicate the remaining 1.5 cents of the state's 10.5- cent-per-gallon gas tax to the Transportation Trust Fund (TTF).

The TTF was established in 1984 by Governor Tom Kean as a means to take control of transportation spending from the legislature. Under the management of Govenor Kean, this mechanism worked as a pay-as-you-go operation.

But it was under Governor Jim Florio that taxpayers saw the beginning of using gas-tax revenue to bond money for expanded projects, such as the failed Camden-Trenton light rail and others like bike paths having nothing to do with reducing traffic.

Assemblyman Michael Patrick Carroll (R-Morristown), was one of several frustrated legislators who were in the minority in opposition to the new borrowing mechanism. Says Carroll,

"Successive Governors borrowed against future revenues, leveraging gas tax revenues through bonding, allowing them to spend more than the current revenues permitted, secure in the knowledge that the bills would come due on their successor's watches. They created a system specifically designed to go bankrupt; in short order, interest and principal payments consume the total gas tax revenue stream. But short-sighted, irresponsible politicians, concerned only with the short-term political benefits attendant to spending, sacrificed the long-term fiscal health of the state on the altar of expedience. They reap the support of grateful spending constituencies, such as unions and contractors, leaving their successors – and the long suffering taxpayers – to deal with the consequences of their profligacy. As we have seen, the result is massive spending on pork projects, the insolvency of the dedicated funds, and the resulting clamor -- from the same spending constituencies which supported the initial profligacy -- for higher taxes and more borrowing."

Carroll is one of the few legislators to openly criticize the reckless and irresponsible actions of the state's government. We need more guys like him.

Voters passed the 2006 ballot question believing the additional revenue would be spent on road improvements. This turned out not to be the case. An examination of the February Transportation Financing Report reveals that the plan was to refinance the existing TTF debt from twenty to thirty years, itself a reckless maneuver, and use the remaining 1.5 cents of the gas tax dedicated to the TTF by passage of the ballot question to borrow approximately $8 billion, without voter approval.

The Trenton financial wizards had found a way to dedicate revenue to the borrowing of another enormous bond issue without the voters ever knowing what hit them. The issuing of these new TTF bonds will bring the state's total debt to over $40 billion, more than the nation of Venezuela.

Christie Whitman is not solely responsible for the financial woes of our state, but she had the chance to begin the painful process of bailing us out. Instead, she punched a hole in the boat, accelerating our plunge toward financial disaster. On financial matters, the emperor has no clothes, and we need politicians and grassroots voter support to demand fiscal responsibility all the way from the town council to the governor's office.

Chapter Eight

The Conservative Mind

"Conservatives have excellent credentials to speak about human rights. By our efforts, and with precious little help from self-styled liberals, we were largely responsible for securing liberty for a substantial share of the world's population and defending it for most of the rest."
--Margaret Thatcher

New Jersey began its conservative history of economic prosperity and freedom at the center of the original thirteen colonies. Launched by a spirit of independence and a willingness to work hard, this state led the nation in economic development from the beginning. That growth and prosperity was born of a heritage of conservative values.

The same conservative thought that inspired Thomas Jefferson and the founders of this great nation to create the Declaration of Independence drove our state's expansion of freedom. When Jefferson penned the opening words to the Declaration, "We hold these truths to be self evident, that all men are created equal, that they are endowed by their creator with certain Unalienable rights. That among these are Life, Liberty and the pursuit of happiness," he rocked governments around the world to their foundations.

Throughout history, every king, queen, emperor, and czar believed that God gave them our rights and they had the power to decide which of these rights and to what extent they would be granted. Jefferson attacked this concept, stating that each and every one of us is given our rights by God and we, the people, decide what power we will give to government - and when such power will be taken away, should that government act irresponsibly.

This fundamental principle is the cornerstone of conservative thought. "Government of the people, by the people and for the people" was the "great experiment" that shocked the rulers of Europe and Asia who thought how brash Americans claim the right to self govern-ment.

To them, this radical conservative plan could never succeed. Like liberals, these rulers did not believe in personal responsibility and the value of the individual, the essence of Jefferson's Declaration. Like liberals, these rulers and dictators believed people need the state for guidance - for the "common good."

Conservatives understand that our nation is built on individual freedom granted by our Creator. By stating this simple fact, Jefferson established that there is no power on earth that can violate "certain unalienable rights." He was not afraid to refer to God in the capacity of a supreme being. He did not claim these rights came from a law journal, special treaty with the king, or a randomly gathered group of protoplasm. Jefferson and the founding fathers unflinchingly stated our rights came from God.

The underlying message to the world was that

nothing on earth could override basic human rights, making them irrevocable by any ruler. To adopt this profound concept and benefit from its protection, however, requires a belief in God. Liberal extremists understand this premise, hence the attack on our Judeo-Christian beliefs and their burning desire to remove God from any corner of government.

It is the government's primary purpose to defend these God-given rights from outside enemies envious of our freedom. This is done by establishing a strong military defense against outside forces and acting as policemen against efforts within our borders that would threaten the rights of any individual. A strong military defense has always been a key point of conservative government and must continue to be a priority. A judicial branch of government committed to defending our basic rights by upholding the constitution, rather than twisting it to implement some politically correct agenda, is the next key element of conservatism. The greatest threat however, is not from outside enemy nations or even terrorists. We can defeat them.

The threat for which we must be always vigilant is the threat of abandoning our core principles of freedom and liberty. The threat of being lulled into complacency and allowing government to take away our God-given rights is ever present and dangerous. Too many quietly follow the course of least resistance and place us all in the hands of a "benevolent" central government promising to provide cradle-to-grave comfort. As shallow-minded liberals promise to dispense compassion, there are those who thoughtlessly slip into a culture of dependency and turn over their individual responsibility for a government funded "affordable housing unit" or "free" daycare.

"Conservative" is one of the most misunderstood, misrepresented, and misused terms in New Jersey politics. Conservatives in this state have failed miserably to express themselves boldly and with sufficient conviction, thereby playing right into the hands of the liberal left. The left relishes proclaiming that conservatives represent narrow-minded ideologies dedicated to failed principles of the past. This image could not be further from the truth

It is the standard, vitriolic rhetoric spewed by the same liberal collectivists and "moderate" Republicans who have engineered the expansion of government dependency so damaging to our culture. Conservatives understand that systematically stealing power from the people and giving it to the government goes against every vital principle in our founding documents. Conservatives know that patriotism is not a dirty word, and that liberty is not an abstract concept to be relegated to quaint, sanitized historical accounts of the events that formed our country.

Liberals will say they are interested in people. Liberals will tell you their interest is in the greater good of humanity, while conservatives are only interested in the protection of the wealthy. They will tell you they are concerned for the poor and downtrodden, the voiceless, and the helpless. But, in actual practice, every policy and precept of their ideology supports the development of a dependent collectivist state and the forfeiture of freedom that is its inevitable consequence.

Much of the blame for the liberal gains made in recent years lies squarely with Republicans. Republican leaders consistently strive to find excuses for their failure to adopt and employ conservative principles. They are afraid to adopt a bold message of freedom and liberty, such as the powerful words of Patrick Henry, when he proclaimed, "Give me liberty or give me death." Many of those who claim to be "conservative" have become apologetic, adopting hyphenated prefixes for their conservatism.

Neo-conservatives, paleo-conservatives, and the "kinder-and-gentler conservatives" of the George Bush Sr. ilk all happily offer up tax increases under some guise of responsible government. Government continues to expand its power. President George Bush's claim to be a compassionate conservative lends credence to the liberal claim that conservatives are not normally compassionate. This qualification of conservative values is never mimicked by liberals. There are no "neo-liberals or "not-so-compassionate liberals," just liberals.

Among conservatives, there is only one hyphenated name I am willing to accept - unapologetic-conservative. I am proud of the principles and commitment of conservative values to this nation.

Liberals today call themselves "progressive" which, in actual practice, means more big-government and expanded entitlement programs. Still others claim to be "reformers," - which ends up meaning nothing, as reformers are most often simply playing on the citizen's frustrations with the current administration.

Reformers will tell you they will make government more efficient or more accountable. "More efficient" translates into taking more of your money faster and spending it quicker. Making government more accountable, in their lexicon, translates as expanded government in the form of taxpayer-funded oversight jobs. Reformers want to be more efficient and accountable about how they spend your money and regulate your freedoms. George Washington Plunkett, boss of the New York Democratic Party during the 18th Century, wrote, "Reformers are morning glories," meaning they ride into office but quickly disappear.

According to liberal ideology, individuals can do nothing for themselves. That's one of the crucial differences between liberals and conservatives. Liberals think the general populace is full of idiots while a select few are smart enough to rule the world. Conservatives know this is a very dangerous trap. A so-called conservative who supports the consolidation of power and growth of government may be many things, but not a conservative. Whether they know it or not, they are helping the cause of creeping socialism.

Liberals win when they cast Republicans as the party of intolerance, the party of ham-fisted military might, the party that hates the little guy. Such attacks from liberal Democrats, combined with the lack of a moral compass within the Republican Party in New Jersey, does great damage to the conservative cause and thus to the Republican Party, whose principles are rooted in conservative philosophy.

These are the conservative ideals of individual liberty and freedom upon which the Founding Fathers established this country. This is the conservative philosophy that released the power of men's minds to develop this state and this country into the greatest and most prosperous economy in history.

Conservatism is not an economic theory, although it has a profound impact on economic development. Conservative thought is diametrically opposed to the liberal elitist doctrine, which strives to blueprint the people's development in every way. Conservatism puts material reward in its proper place and has a structured view of individuals and their role in society. Economics is a factor, but only plays a subordinate role. The conservative considers the whole person while the liberal looks only at the material side of man's nature. Conservatives value a person's spiritual growth as vital to our society and economics as a means to facilitate that growth. Freedom, liberty, individual responsibility, and accountability are at the center of this spiritual existence.

Liberals, on the other hand, view satisfaction of economic wants as the primary mission of society. They seek to harness society's political and economic forces into a collective effort to compel "progress" under the yoke of one-size-fits-all egalitarianism. As any woman shopping for a dress can tell you, one-size-fits-all actually fits no one. To liberals, individual advancement is the enemy, so money is redistributed through taxation. Educational standards are lowered so no one feels unfairly challenged and everyone gets the same sub-standard quality of health care.

This insidious effort flies in the face of human nature. The basic instincts of individuals are to break free, excel, and improve the situation for themselves and their families, each to the best of his or her individual ability.

During the Cold War, it was almost amusing to see Russian athletes awarded medals at the Olympics – an award which should symbolize personal achievement. When interviewed, the team leaders were always quick to assert that the medal was for Mother Russia and Mother Russia alone. No matter how hard they tried, they couldn't mask the one dead giveaway - the look of personal pride in the eyes of the winner. It is human nature to want to succeed, to compete, and to be recognized for one's success. Liberals find this type of personal success abhorrent because in their world view everything is luck of the draw.

The first obligation of those seeking to be political leaders should be to understand the nature of man. In doing so, the true conservative thinker can gain knowledge from the wisdom of the ancient philosophers, drawing from the brilliant thinking of Aristotle, who said, "In the arena of human life the honors and rewards fall to those who show their good qualities..."[1] and "The basis of a Democratic state is liberty..."[2] Later philosophers like John Locke continued the tradition. Locke said, "Good

---

1   Aristotle, Nicomachean Ethics, 4th c. BC
2   Aristotle, Politics

and evil, reward and punishment, are the only motives to a rational creature: these are the spur and reins whereby all mankind are set on work, and guided..."[3] This thinking culminated in Thomas Jefferson's Declaration of the pure virtue of individual liberty.

While conservatives do not claim to have a monopoly on learning, we are not too proud to learn from the great minds of the past. The first thing a conservative understands is that each person is a unique, individual member of the species. Only a philosophy that takes into account the individual differences between members of its society can provide an environment in which these differences can develop the individual potential of each person. Only in this way can true freedom and liberty be offered as a society's greatest virtue.

As a definition, a conservative is anyone who believes that government should be as small as possible, the military should be strong, the Constitution protected and upheld, and power should belong in the hands of the people.

We hear much from the liberal left about the need for expanded social programs, such as the "Paid Family Leave" bill. This bill, proposed by the Corzine Administration, will provide pay for workers to take time off to provide "psychological comfort" to a family member. This new entitlement has been copied from the socialist handbook adopted by countries like Cuba and North Korea. Like so many liberal initiatives, this bill claims to "be compassionate."

The term compassion has been hijacked as a liberal mantra that replaces sound thinking and reason with emotion. Funded by another tax, this new income redistribution scheme expands the culture of dependency while claiming to support the "common man" and to ex-

---

3   Locke, John, Some Thought Concerning Education, The Harvard Classics, Section 54

ist for the "common good."

Liberals have adopted the concept of the "common good" as a trendy title for sacrificing the individual. This term first emerged as the basis of thinking of Red China's Chairman Mao Tse-tung and even in the speeches of Stalin. The term has found its way into American politics in recent years as a catch-all phrase to justify every new government program and spending plan.

During his January 9, 2007 State of the State address, Governor Jon Corzine referred to the "common good" 12 times. The terms freedom and liberty were never used. The "common good" is a concept that pays little attention to the history of a nation forged from the efforts of uncommon men whose uncommon vision and risks have gifted mankind with a beacon of freedom and liberty. Two centuries later, this beacon still draws people from around the world yearning for opportunity.

The conservative recognizes replacing individual freedom with the "common good" means sacrificing the individual. The result is people are to be tossed into an undifferentiated mass and relegated to debilitating dependency. The conservative understands that the economic and spiritual aspects of a man's nature are intertwined. A man who is dependent on the state for his economic needs cannot be free to excel. Our state and country will only achieve optimum growth and prosperity when every individual is free to reach his or her highest potential.

The conservative knows that a person's development, both economically and spiritually, is something that cannot be determined by outside forces without damaging the individual. All individuals, for their own good and for the good of society, must be free to make, and responsible for, their own choices. If you help a baby chick struggling to get out of its shell, the baby chick dies because the struggle was the only thing which has the power to give it the strength to live. Reliance on government programs promulgated by the liberal collectivists serves to rob the individual of the initiative and determination required to meet the challenges of life. This reduces individuals to becoming nameless faces identified by a Social Security number, with no motivation to work or excel at any aspect of their meager lives.

Liberalism is a political manifesto encompassing social objectives that consign individuals to obscurity as part of the huddled masses. It is a manifesto that rejects the inviolability of our most cherished constitutional precepts at both the federal and state levels. It calls for a "living constitution" that, over time, will allow ongoing mutation of the fundamental principles protected by our vital documents.

Unchallenged, liberal collectivism will lead inexorably toward totalitarianism, which marks the death knell of the American Dream. To defend that Dream and the future of the fundamental rights so hard fought for in the American Revolution and afterwards, one must return to and fully understand the ideology of conservatism and its roll in building this nation. Words matter and the words of the Founders captured with brevity the most fundamental concepts of freedom, liberty and conservative thought.

Adopting these simple concepts gives the conservative thinker a full set of values. To understand them and defend them takes a lot more study. To explain these concepts, we must return to the observations of Thomas Jefferson and Thomas Paine.

"We are endowed by our Creator with certain unalienable rights." Man is endowed by a natural desire to be free. This basic human instinct must be allowed to exist and, even more so, it must be able to catapult the individual to greater heights, and bring those who benefit along. The liberal seeks to keep all society at the same level. They call it "unfair" if one person or group prospers and believe those who lag behind are entitled to a mortgage on the success of others. There are numerous examples of this destructive force, the Mount Laurel Doctrine being one of the most offensive. The lowering of education standards in New Jersey to accommodate more students is another.

"Amongst them life, liberty and the pursuit of happiness." Every man must exist for his own sake under the auspices of "enlightened self-interest." This recognizes the good of the whole while pursuing personal gain. No one is coerced to sacrifice himself to others nor are others coerced to sacrifice themselves to him. The pursuit of enlightenment is in his own self-interest and his own happiness is the highest moral purpose of his life. For the religious man, enlightened self-interest includes love of others as proof of his love of God, but this caring for the needs of others and the resulting redistribution of income, is voluntary and not extracted under threat from the government.

"All men are created equal." The liberal left confuses equality under the law with one-size-fits-all equality, or egalitarianism. This flawed social system penalizes those that are successful and establishes the concept that those that are not have a right to the success of others. Those who adopt the welfare state as their keeper are taught to believe they have a mortgage on the prosperity of those who are the producers. This liberal mentality has so negatively impacted the ability of those who produce to prosper that they are leaving New Jersey to seek economic freedom elsewhere. As the liberal collectivists cannot continue to finance their failed social programs on the backs of those leaving, liberal Governor Jon Corzine will determine what road to take: individual liberty or the "common good."

"Give me liberty or give me death. Governments

are instituted among Men, deriving their just powers from the consent of the governed." The ideal political economic system is laissez faire capitalism. This is the only system where men deal with one another, not as tyrants and subjects or expropriators and victims, but as traders engaged in free voluntary exchange for mutual benefit. It is a system where no man can expropriate from another by physical or political force and no man may initiate the use of physical or political force against others. The government acts only as a policeman that protects man's rights. The government only uses force against those who have initiated force against its citizens, such as criminals or foreign invaders. The use of political force against its citizens is prohibited by constitutional restraints and representatives elected to a republic form of government.

Capitalism, as synthesized and crystallized in the United States, is responsible for the explosion of economic development in New Jersey. As an economic engine, its success is unparalleled in world history. From origins in Europe in the 16th to 19th centuries, capitalism evolved into a political philosophy in our founding documents, stating clearly that man's right to his own life, to his own liberty, and to the pursuit of his own happiness is a God-given right for every individual.

This is America's implicit moral code, but it was not sufficiently explicit in formulation to ensure protection within the confines of our Constitution nor has it been unfailingly upheld by a Supreme Court that refuses to fulfill a sacred oath to enforce those protections. The Founding Fathers knew this; the very freedoms protected by the Constitution provide the tools for its dilution and unmaking.

New Jersey's economic base and dynamic social fabric is deteriorating for lack of a conservative, capitalist, moral base. The destructive force is the morality of socialism, which holds that no man has the right to exist for his own sake and service to others is the only moral justification for his existence. Self-sacrifice, coerced if necessary, is his highest moral duty. The political expression of socialism is collectivism, the rampant governmental expansionism that has permeated our statehouse and which holds that man's life and work belong to the state, the group, the gang, the "common good." The state may expropriate whatever it deems necessary for its own tribal collective "common good." Those in power get to define what "common good" means in that context, proving again that power corrupts.

Capitalism and socialism cannot coexist within the same man or in the same society. The conflict is now reaching its climax in New Jersey, resulting in the massive outward migration of residents and the steady decline of our once envied economy. The choice is clear. We can choose to return our state to the free-market capitalist system with limited government, and its consequences of freedom, justice, progress, and happiness. Or, we can accept the primordial morality of liberalism.

New Jersey government must abandon its interference in the state's economy and adopt a policy of separation of economy and state for the same reasons liberals scream for separation of church and state.

Throughout history, true conservatives have been at war with tyrants and democratic promulgators of extreme revolutionary opinions. The conservative is as angered by those under the yoke of Islamic fundamentalist domination as he is by those that parade under the banner of one-size-fits-all equality. The conservative opposes any effort to debase the dignity and autonomy of the individual. We are at odds with not just dictators, but also those quiet collectivists who wish to manipulate individuals through social programs.

Conservatives understand the primary role of

government is to preserve freedom. We know that government, as it grows, becomes a self-aggrandizing entity with unlimited appetite. Conservatives know it is necessary and incumbent upon every individual to be vigilant in defense of our freedoms, as there are those who will sacrifice these freedoms in the name of the common good.

Good motives are not sufficient. The worst socialist failures all began with the best of intentions. Consider the movements of the last century. The civil rights movement, predicated on equal rights and equal treatment under the law, degenerated into a clamorous special interest feeding frenzy demanding racial preferences and minority set asides. The sexual revolution, less laudable but ostensibly about personal freedom, rotted into epidemics of herpes and AIDS and rampant internet pornography. The peace movement weakened our military, encouraged tyrants near and far, and undermined our resolve in foreign policy. Feminists entered the latter half of the 20th Century championing unrestricted abortion, which now includes the barbaric practice of partial birth abortion, and the "freedom" of teenage girls to get an abortion – a dangerous medical procedure – without the requirement of parental consent.

Throughout the history of this country, conservatives have recognized the need to be ever vigilant. We have asked and will continue to ask: "Are we doing everything in our power to protect and promote freedom?" In this commitment true conservatives remain steadfast, unlike those who support the creeping social decay that is the inevitable result of the liberal movement. We must continue to be committed to preserving economic and individual freedom and government of the people, by the people, and for the people every step of the way.

Chapter Nine

The Disgrace of Activist Judges

*"Judges are like umpires. Umpires don't make the
rules; they apply them."*
--Chief Justice John Roberts

Liberal Democrats and "moderate" Republicans
routinely rely on liberal judges to advance their agendas.
Unable to take voter's "no" as an answer, liberals seek
out legal ways to do an end-run around them, and more
often than not get a pass from a biased press. When ques-
tioned, these politicians offer some glib reply to disguise
their position as being best for the "common good," while
blatantly shifting power out of the hands of the people.

Take a look at the Mount Laurel case that forces
low income housing into every single New Jersey town.
Consider the *Robinson* and *Abbott* school funding cases
where taxpayers are obligated to never ending and always increasing subsidies to reach unattainable and un-
realistic education goals. Or evaluate the *Right to Choose
v. Byrne* case by which the court somehow established a
Constitutional right to a taxpayer-funded abortion.

And those cases are just the tip of the iceberg. In a

series of cases I personally filed and raised money to support, our Supreme Court termed the Constitutional Debt Limitation Clause a dead letter. They have thwarted application of the death penalty even in the most extreme of cases and stopped the State Police from using established, effective criminal profiling procedures. These pro-criminal court decisions are a direct reason that crime in our state is on the rise once again after years of reductions.

Voters' rights, local control of our communities and defense of our values have all been eroded by this unholy alliance of black-robed oligarchs and elected officials who have no regard for taxpayer rights let alone the conservative principles that have built this country. The courts have taken their power too far: now it's time for people to fight back.

Many of our friends have given up the fight. Our former New Jersey neighbors, now living in Florida, Texas, Tennessee or Nevada - all states with no state income tax - or even those who moved across the border to Pennsylvania where top income tax rates are barely a third of those here, voted with their feet. Their wealth and knowledge is now lost to our state.

Meanwhile New Jersey attracts freeloaders and laggards seeking the most generous government handouts in the country whether in the form of direct welfare giveaways or lavish government jobs loaded with benefits private sector employers can only dream of providing their employees. Homeless people seeking one of Governor Jon Corzine's 100,000 low income apartments will be forced into towns like yours. And the proposed new Paid Family Leave law will attract even more people looking for a free ride at someone else's expense - that "someone else" being you and me and the rest of the good taxpayers of New Jersey.

Despite all of this, I still believe New Jersey can be saved from the gang of government-employee unions, trial lawyers, pseudo-intellectuals, social engineers and urban politicians currently destroying our state. I wrote this book because I refuse to throw in the towel, and if enough people feel the same way New Jersey can be rehabilitated and once again be a state that attracts jobs, not repels them, that stands up for working families instead of welfare recipients. New Jersey can be a place where hard-working families can achieve the American Dream of owning their own home, thereby bypassing the nightmare of renting a cheap one from Governor Jon Corzine.

The Old Route 1 Bridge linking New Jersey and Pennsylvania has a neon sign that still reads "Trenton Makes -- The World Takes." But in recent years that slogan would better read "New Jersey Makes -- Trenton Takes." New Jersey cannot survive if we continue down the current liberal path both political parties have carried us down.

Several years ago, the South Orange-Maplewood Board of Education ordered that Christmas carols and even instrumental Christmas music could not be played at Maplewood's Columbia High School "Winter Concert" or anywhere else on campus. I found this an egregious and offensive position, so I organized an "illegal" Christmas carol sing-along in front of Columbia High School on the same night of the atheistic pagan ceremony sponsored by the taxpayer-funded school board. I drove down with a few members from my church and a group of Orthodox Jews from Teaneck.

The sun had long set by the time we arrived at 5 pm and, as we turned the corner, visions of ACLU picket lines danced in my head. To my delighted surprise, when we arrived, we were greeted by a group of nearly 100 mostly African-American students who had heard about what we were going to do and joined us. The event turned out to be a major success, both in terms of turnout and the message we put forth.

It was very heartening to see that the fight against political correctness had such broad support, but what really shocked me was how people reacted to what we did. As I did radio and television interviews both locally and across the country, people seemed amazed that someone would actually stand up against the forces of political correctness in favor of what is right.

The response to the plan was an overwhelming outcry of national support and a sudden awareness that we as "one nation under God" had replaced Merry Christmas with Happy Holidays. The Christmas season had become some sort of marketing mush that had nothing to do with our faith or Jesus Christ. The school board's ruling was a foolish attempt to squelch freedom of speech and artistic expression in an effort to appease a tiny minority who claimed to be offended by religious songs. These individuals, if they even existed, were not required to sit and listen to any songs they did not like. These narrow-minded bigots even wanted to stop the playing of Bach's "Joy to the World" an instrumental tune with no lyrics.

Their argument is the party line for all radical liberal secularists who want only to wipe out any vestige of the Judeo-Christian heritage on which our nation was founded. Their motivation is not driven by the quest for freedom or caring for their fellow man, but by hatred for Judeo-Christian values of faith, family, and freedom, and Christians in particular. It is intellectually bankrupt to claim that students in a learning environment cannot share music and even ideas of faith. This is antithetical to learning and understanding and good old-fashioned entertainment. If this minority of anti-American extremists hate our fundamental beliefs so much and are so offended they would rob the vast majority of us from enjoying our faiths and freedoms they should move to Cuba. They can sit there in drab clothes and a substandard dwelling and rejoice in paying homage to Fidel's socialist state instead of God.

Cultural stability is an arena in which the battle is waged. If the foundations can be sufficiently assailed by the far left – by promoting rights of criminals, a culture of death, and a zeitgeist of godless despair, they can take over the government and undertake their socialist utopia in earnest.

The Thread that Binds Us

In June of 2006, Bogota came face-to-face with the nation's growing debate over the importance of the English language to the stability of our culture. The McDonald's Corporation, the world's largest food service company with sales of $53 billion, made the marketing determination that the way to promote their business in Bogota was to post billboards in only Spanish. This decision would pitch me head-to-head with McDonald's' U.S. Division President Ralph Alvarez and the entire bilingual movement. The firestorm of debate once again revealed the ultra-liberal agenda of the New Jersey Supreme Court and the lack of principle of leading Republicans on an issue fundamental to our society.

The saga began June 3rd when McDonald's posted a billboard promoting their iced coffee on River Road in Bogota. What made this billboard unique was that it was entirely in Spanish. Bogota has a growing Latino population, but the vast majority of our residents speak English.

The 2001 federal census reported less than 1% of our population could not speak English. Bogota has always been a diverse community. Dutch settlers were followed by Germans, Polish, Irish, and Italians. Those who had migrated to our town were often new immigrants or first-generation Americans whose families spoke another language at home. The heritage of this community, like most of America, was to strive to be Americans. Bogota has always been proud to be part of the great melting pot that is created through the adoption of English as our common language.

In The Federalist Papers #2 John Jay wrote "these thirteen loosely knit colonies are bound together by one thread -- our common English language..." This principle had been understood in Bogota until McDonald's drove a wedge into our community and brought a simmering national debate to a boil.

On the first day the billboard was installed I received several calls and comments from residents asking what was happening in Bogota. Comments like "When did this start?" and "Who's taking over our town?" were typical. I realized this billboard was stirring up resentment towards our growing Latino population and unnecessarily so. The Latino population of Bogota had not asked McDonald's for this billboard. We don't even have a McDonald's in town. The adjoining town of Ridgefield Park where the road on which the billboard stands leads doesn't have a McDonald's. I decided to call the billboard company and ask them what their rationale was for the location for this message.

Viacom Corp. was the outdoor advertising agency that had placed the billboard. I contacted the regional sales manager and asked him why this billboard had been located in Bogota. He told me that it had been a mistake and that the company's placement department had made an error. These billboards were meant for four towns in Hudson and Essex Counties with large non-English speaking Latino populations. He said the sign would be replaced with an English version. That should have been the end of the story, but enter stage left the typical angry feminist liberal attorney.

The Record newspaper reporter Brian Aberback,

contacted me about the billboard after he found out I had asked Viacom to have it removed. He told me the attorney for Viacom told him the billboard would not be removed. I contacted Viacom and was immediately confronted with vitriol as I was greeted condescendingly with "Well, mayor, do you have a problem with the image of Iced Coffee?" Upon my denial of this bizarre question she followed with "Do you have a problem with the Spanish language?" Any attempt to explain my concern was drowned in the mindless anger of liberal self-righteousness.

The conversation concluded with the Viacom representative declaring she would be contacting the ACLU and abruptly hanging up. As her braying faded from my ears, I found it flattering to think that McDonald's Corporation and its endless line of attorneys would need to run to the ACLU for protection from the mayor of the little old borough of Bogota.

While the threat of ACLU involvement was reported in the press, to my disappointment it never came to pass. Even the ACLU realized we had not interfered in the First Amendment rights of McDonald's; we had simply made a request that McDonald's respect the borough's heritage and perhaps engender through their marketing plan a respect for the fundamental principle that English is the language of prosperity and the future of our country. McDonald's should realize that in promulgating bilingualism they are empowering the left-wing that sees bilingualism as one more arrow to the heart of our democracy. The left doesn't look at a swelling Hispanic population and think of them as another wave of immigrants seeking opportunity. Instead, they see a poor, disenfranchised voting bloc, which if they can be courted the right way will vote Democratic.

Conspicuous in their absence, Republicans or Democrats were nowhere to be found on this issue. This is an issue that has been debated since the beginning of our nation's history, but in today's world of appeasement and the lack of courage that has reduced the Republican Party in New Jersey to the role of lackeys sniffing around for political patronage crumbs, the Republican Party choose to ignore this vital issue. Most Republicans in New Jersey are scared to death to take a strong, principled position for fear of being called "racists."

For 230 years Americans have debated this issue and consistently come down on the side of being a monolingual, English-speaking country. During the Louisiana Purchase President James Madison declared English the official language of the new territory ending a long, heated argument over French or English. Democrats are catering to the growing Latino population by promoting bilingualism and assuming it will buy them votes. They are mistaken. The average Latino immigrant understands the importance of the English language and wants to learn the language of their adoptive country, just like all the immigrant populations that have preceded them.

I saw this same lack of rational thinking when as a candidate for Governor, I called a news conference on Martin Luther King Day on Martin Luther King Jr. Blvd. in Newark to declare that as Governor, I would issue an executive order ending all state programs that use race instead of merit. Inevitably, the same gang of race hustlers called me a racist and asked how dare I make such a proclamation on such a hallowed day – these are the same people who think MLK Day should be a holiday but Christmas should not.

I pointed out that it was Dr. King himself who had a dream that men and women should be judged "on the content of their character, not the color of their skin." But this is of no consequence to the race-baiting demagogues who call the shots in today's politically correct world. Logic and reason are not useful, only what preserves the established status quo where liberal special interests rule at the top of the heap. What is right is irrelevant and to these people, wrong.

The McDonald's billboard debacle highlighted the need for voters of New Jersey to be heard. The Republicans had run for the hills and Democrats were pandering to the left-wing bilingual lobby. The media had a field day attacking my request that McDonald's remove their sign. The letters and emails I received, however, ran three-to-one in my favor.

It seemed to me this was a conservative issue on which people should have the right to express their opinion in an open Democratic process. The ballot box was the perfect place for voters to speak out. Twenty-seven states have passed referendums establishing English as their official language. This law requires that all state or town records, minutes of meetings, laws, and various application forms be maintained in English. There are practical exceptions for documents that may impact public health or safety and in cases were access to fair judiciary proceedings is at stake. This is a practical measure as it establishes a standard for doing business that is fair and equal for everyone. It eliminates the political decision as to whether or not to provide foreign language documents to one group and not another.

On June 15 the Bogota borough council - with a bipartisan majority of both Democrats and Republicans - placed this question on the ballot for our voters to decide. New Jersey does not have Initiative and Referendum that would allow voters to petition to put a question on the ballot, but Bogota does! Our state legislature could have put this question on the ballot but the legislature refuses to do so as it would not pass their test of political correctness. This question was ripe for a vote and Bogota voters were excited about the chance to debate the issue and be heard.

But the opportunity to exercise true democracy was taken away by a so-called Republican, Bergen County Clerk Kathleen Donovan, and the infamous liberal activist New Jersey Supreme Court. Donovan received the legal paperwork required to place the question on the ballot well before the deadline, but on the eve of finalizing the ballot she had her attorney Jack Carbone notify the Borough of Bogota that she would not allow our voters the right to vote on making English their official language. Twenty-seven states had voted on this identical law and until that time not one American had been denied the right to vote on this question. Donovan had her own idea of voters' rights and the value of the English language, and in her effort to pander to a liberal, politically correct constituency, she decided that her views trumped the right of the people to vote.

Donovan is a liberal Republican and self-described "progressive" who once described herself as "pro-labor, pro-choice, pro-gun control and pro-affirmative action."

It shouldn't have been to anyone's surprise that she would use her role as Clerk to promote a liberal ideology she obviously so strongly supports. Her decision to steal Bogota voters' right to be part of the Democratic process was based on her claim that it would be "unconstitutional" to make English our official language because it would violate someone's "freedom of speech."

Donovan, who initiated bilingual ballots in Bergen County before being forced to do so by federal law had either not read the law or didn't care what it said. The case went to the state Supreme Court and to no one's surprise the court treated the case with contempt, upholding the Clerk's misuse of her authority in taking a non-binding referendum question off the ballot. For the first time in American history citizens would be denied the right to vote on establishing English as their official language because it didn't line up with the personal prejudices of a few appointed officials.

This is another example of the Republican Party's failure to stand on principle, afraid to take a stand as they shudder in fear of being called "racists." Like a lifeguard watching a swimmer drown, mumbling quietly to himself, "gee, that's too bad" the Republicans stood asleep at the switch while an arrogant bureaucrat turned democracy on its head.

Party hacks don't understand that average voters do not root for political parties like they do a football game between the Shirts and Skins. Those of us who believe in Republican and conservative principles will not vote for any jerk with an "R" before their name. Yet party bosses continue to be surprised when their candidates lose because disgusted, disenfranchised conservatives stay home. This loss of freedom has been visited on us by a Republican elected official and the New Jersey Supreme Court - a majority of whose members were appointed by Republican governors.

Is anyone surprised Republicans have lost control in New Jersey?

Chapter Ten

An Epoch Battle

Pundits decry daily that New Jersey is a hopelessly liberal state. This comes as a result of a series of losses relegating New Jersey to the control of the Democratic Party and the neutering of Republicans. Yes, I said neutering Republicans, who stand quaking in their proverbial boots at the thought of promoting a bold conservative agenda, unable to articulate that vision for this state's future.

Ronald Reagan won twice here and George Bush Sr. won his first term, before violating his famous "no new taxes" pledge. Only seven years ago, Republicans had control of the Governor's office, the Assembly, and Senate until they, too, abandoned the foundation principles of conservatism that defines the Republican Party. In the wake of these failures, a consequence of the fatal collapse of ideas and principles that built this country, the liberal socialist agenda of Governor Jon Corzine advances unfettered.

Throughout modern history, there has raged a battle between the principles of the individual and the dogma of the collectivist state. The battle ahead in New

Jersey is not just about who will run the Trenton machine. Republicans versus Democrats must become more than a "shirts versus the skins" competition to see whose club will be in charge of dividing the spoils of political warfare. The real confrontation is an epochal battle of principles and will determine the future of New Jersey's development as either an enclave of freedom and liberty or a government manipulated collectivist state, where the individual is cast into an amorphous mass of humanity and relegated to obscurity.

Republicans must be prepared to stand forth with a bold vision for New Jersey's future. They will have to advance an argument against the entitlement programs that are perpetuating a society of learned dependence and return to a heritage of personal responsibility. This vision must be rooted in the beliefs of the founders and derived from hundreds of years of learning. For New Jersey to prosper and grow, we must shed ourselves of the burden of ever growing government and the consequence of a diminishing economy.

The pundits who claim the people of New Jersey are more liberal seem to believe residents of our state have inherited different brain cells than our neighbors across the border in Pennsylvania or friends who have moved to Florida to seek lower taxes. Perhaps they believe those moving into our state are seeking the opportunity to live in the state with the highest taxes in the nation, when in actuality the state's greatest draw is its expanded entitlement programs, including the nation's most "progressive" low income housing scheme.

The reality is the Republican Party has failed to offer a sound argument and firm commitment to conservative principles and, therefore, have allowed the liberal machine to advance with little or no opposition. Republican legislators have adopted an "every man for himself" approach that sets principles and values aside for the purpose of winning their own elections, even when that means abandoning the most basic tenets of Republicanism. There is no clear and bold Republican message because the leadership of the Republican Party is in a shambles and unable to rally the voters and generate excitement about their vision.

To this end, the Republicans have turned our state over to the philosophy, not of Thomas Jefferson, but of Governor Jon Corzine's childhood hero Dag Hammarskjold[1] - the father of planned central government and a proud advocate of the socialist state. The intellectual vacuum left by the Republican abandonment of conservatism has been readily filled by principled liberals as committed to their big government vision as real conservatives are to the belief in freedom.

The people of New Jersey deserve a choice. They are hungry for leadership that will conquer rising taxes and skyrocketing debt. Our citizens feel the pain of the changes in our economic decline, as high taxes drive their neighbors away and wage growth fails to keep pace with the nation. New Jersey residents fear their property rights are threatened by eminent domain abuse and that their children's education is not competitive with world standards. Their disgust is reflected in the outward migration of taxpayers in all tax brackets as the liberal administration works to repopulate our state through a government mandated, taxpayer funded, low income housing program that would be the envy of Lenin.

The goal of conservatives is to make New Jersey a magnet state for those seeking freedom and prosperity, not those stretching out their hands for a government entitlement. A hand up, not a hand out, is what builds a prosperous society. A free, prosperous economy does more to promulgate opportunity than any government

---

1   During Governor Corzine's State of the State Address, February 22, 2007, he states Dag is his childhood hero.

program in history.

Republicans need to remember that basic truth and not be afraid to promote its virtues. Republicans must create a "handbook" for victory and not cower in the face of liberal opposition when their opponents decry their lack of "compassion." Liberals will attack Republicans, who should be calling for cutting the size of government, saying we "need" government programs to survive. They will be the first to smirk when Republicans capitulate to their demands and then continue their call for more funding to expand their collectivist state. The strength to stand up to this onslaught can only come from strong leadership that equips the team with sound and principled arguments.

The agenda Republicans need to win and, most of all, to govern effectively can be defined by returning to the core values that built this nation. Conservative principles will resonate in this state if delivered with conviction and outlined in such a way that makes clear to each voter that their individuality and prosperity is at the forefront of consideration when government is in the hands of conservatives. To accomplish that end, Conservative Republicans should have an orchestrated message in every legislative district across the state.

A district with more minorities, or union workers, is as concerned with individual freedom as any other. Pandering to black voters in Newark based on some ridiculous belief these voters are looking for more expanded government programs will never help Republicans. Even big spending Republicans cannot win with this nonsense. Black voters in Newark and Camden cherish their individuality and freedoms as much as, or even more so, than suburban voters, white or black.

The tool that offers prosperity to those trapped in failed inner cities is school vouchers. Republicans should lead the effort to break the hold of union bosses on these school systems and give the parents the chance to control their children's education with the same opportunities the children of Bill Clinton and Al Gore had attending private schools in Washington DC.

Republicans should stand on their conservative message and get back to basics. Paramount to winning elections, Republicans must govern like conservatives, remembering they cannot make a contract with America and then break that contract. They cannot create a constitution and then ignore it, and we cannot endorse a Bill of Rights and then say those rights are wrong. The defense of liberty does not come easily and it begins in the chambers of the Statehouse.

The Republican pledge to New Jersey should call for a return to limited government, starting with reestablishing the Debt Limitation Clause of the constitution and returning the right to vote to our citizens. The gutting of this constitutional protection and its ensuing explosion of non voter authorized debt has led to an unprecedented expansion of central government.

The Republican Party must call for an amendment to the Constitution establishing this clause as inviolable and assert that no violation of this fundamental right can be bypassed by some judicial initiative that the black-robed oligarchs determine is so vital that voters' rights must be violated. We have witnessed the destruction the liberal activists judiciary has caused in their call for school construction funding in the rampant corruption of the School Construction Corporation. The voters of New Jersey will support this amendment by an overwhelming majority.

Conservatives must call for the dismantling of the states' behemoth bureaucracy and devolve control to local governments. Preservation of Home Rule should be at the heart of the Republican platform. The argument for local control of neighborhoods, schools and, most important, our own lives, is sound. The facts about the efficiency of small, local government and its advantages to defending liberty should be inculcated in every Republican message. If this simple message is repeated in newspaper editorials, radio talk shows, debates and speeches around the state and backed up with facts - voters will respond because the truth is - small is better.

The facts and the spirit of community win the day in any debate as the collectivist agenda is exposed. It is more difficult to support this premise when many Republicans have sipped the collectivist Kool-Aid. But, from the ancient writing of Aristotle to the practical management models of today's successful businesses, the benefits of decentralized control are overwhelmingly apparent. For Republicans to lead, they need to advance individuality and the desire of those individuals to self-govern and maintain and exercise control over their neighborhoods.

The greatest obstacle to the liberal agenda is local government. Liberals know that, if they are going to implement their social engineering scheme, including state-wide government housing, a centralized education system and every other collectivist program, they must weaken local government to the point of ineffectiveness.

Liberal Democrat leaders also recognize that small suburban communities are clusters of reliable Republican votes. Building high-density "transit villages" in the Republican communities in the Highlands District, for example, will move large concentrations of Democrats into these once solidly Republican territories. At the base of this rallying cry is a simple slogan - New Jersey residents need less "state" and more "town."

Conservative Republicans are equipped to attack the worst income tax structure in the United States. In 2004, Governor Jim McGreevey raised the top rate to 8.97%, claiming this would "guarantee" tax relief for seniors. Instead, we have seen the flight of high income residents and a further intensification of the redistribution of wealth from the suburbs to the failed inner city school districts.

The so-called "Property Tax Relief Fund" is nothing more than a tool for the state to take control of our once outstanding education system and put it in the hands of the Trenton bureaucracy. The Republican Party has the opportunity to take a vital leadership position that will redirect the course of education in this state for the better by attacking the Abbott decision head on.

Conservatives should be calling meetings across the state, whenever and wherever possible, promoting the effort to overturn this failed liberal policy and return education to parents by calling for the equal distribution of the "Property Tax Relief Fund" on a per student basis.

It must be required that any school district that cannot produce a quality education with this funding, combined with a local property tax contribution, will have to give parents a voucher for their children to attend the schools of their choice. This will require the courage to take on the vested interests, including the NJEA Teacher's Union and the Newark Teacher's Union.

This is the single most important battle taxpayers and students can fight in the years to come. Republicans have the chance to be at the vanguard of this critical fight, or they can cut and run, as they have been doing. The financial benefit to taxpayers of equal funding for each student is an average 20% property tax cut for all suburban property taxpayers. Over the long run, the income tax could be reduced and even eliminated as efficiencies are gained and bureaucracies eliminated.

Republicans must stand for, commit to, work for, and succeed in CUTTING TAXES. Small insignificant tax cuts are not good enough. Republicans must call for and implement sweeping cuts in the size of government through downsizing, prioritizing and privatizing government services. Republicans should call for the elimination of all new government departments established in the last ten years and every job added to the state's bloated payroll.

In the on-going drive to grow Trenton's massive bureaucracy, Governor Corzine signed a bill establishing the new layer of bureaucracy called the "Office of the Comptroller." This powerful $9 million enforcement arm of the governor's office will be charged with auditing the auditors. One unnecessary patronage mill, the Department of Community Affairs Division of Local Government Services, is already armed with the authority to audit local municipal budgets. New Jersey is the only state that requires budget oversight of local governments for the purpose of "preventive" measures. In other words, New Jersey has more central government intrusion, regulations, mandates, and bureaucracy than any other state.

Four years ago, McGreevey established the State Office of "Inspector General" to root out waste and corruption. Then we heard about the Department of the Public Advocate to root out waste and corruption. Now we are told this new layer of bureaucracy will root out waste and corruption.

This job pool will be the mechanism used to force local municipalities to implement the Corzine agenda. This police force will add more confusion and delays in management of municipal governments as the Trenton establishment puts Project Labor Agreements, Mount Laurel requirements, minority set asides, an endless list of unfunded mandates, and Department of Environmental Protection regulations ahead of the interests of property taxpayers.

This is another step in the on-going movement towards centralization of power in a state government that has already proven reckless and irresponsible. The result of this collectivist agenda has been manifested in the loss of voter's rights to approve new debt, the centralization of control of education, the override of local zoning by the Mount Laurel Doctrine, and massive income redistribution. We can't afford more layers of government. There is a lot more at risk than higher taxes, as if that isn't bad enough. We are witnessing the loss of our property rights to eminent domain abuse, the over regulation of our businesses and the loss of home rule to a band of nameless, faceless bureaucrats in Trenton.

All of these departments should go - they are nothing more than layers of bureaucracy that accomplish nothing. They will never achieve a thing for taxpayers that justify their creation and Republicans should say so with conviction. The newly created State Department of Economic Planning should be eliminated immediately, and with a not so fond farewell. This Corzine initiative is directly from the socialist handbook, and is so contrary to the free market principles that have powered this state, it is insulting to every supporter of free market philosophy.

Every well known free market economist, from Nobel Prize winner Friedrich Hayek to Ludwig von Mises, has stated that central to advancement of a socialist agenda is the establishment of a department of central economic planning. This was Governor Jon Corzine's first new department, formed after the passage of the 2006-2007 budgets. This central planning bureau serves as the traffic cops for income redistribution and the planners for every social engineering scheme coming out of Trenton.

These departments should be the first to go and there are plenty more. One of the greatest challenges to a new conservative administration is the closing of a department or elimination of a program. There is no manual on how to close a department of government. The concept of "downsizing" sounds good in a speech, but in real practice is difficult. It requires goring someone else's bull and taking on establishments that will fight tooth and nail for survival and protection of their government benefits. The electorate knows this through subtle intuition.

When the battle rages on television with picket lines and boisterous public meetings, the voters tuning in understand their representatives are finally making the tough decisions they promised in campaign speeches. Most of the time, however, these elected officials become wrapped up in the moment and, under the pressure of a loud and organized minority, they fold like cheap suitcases. Republicans should campaign on a bold plan to reduce government, cut taxes, and put control in the hands of the people. Upon the victory that is the inevitable result of such bold leadership, they must move into office with a blueprint for change ready to be implemented with decisive and rapid strokes.

At the base of this philosophy is a belief that money should be kept in the pockets of taxpayers. They've earned it and the government should take only the bare minimum necessary to run the few services we require from our government. Downsizing should reflect a return to basic services. Prioritizing should be analyzing and reestablishing just what we expect our state government to be responsible for, such as state roads, courts and state police. Privatization relies on the understanding that the private sector is far more capable and efficient at performing almost every task the government requires.

At the center of the rights of Americans lies the right to own one's property free of threat that the government can take it away. Serfs of old possessed their land at the whim of the King and struggled under the threat of loss at any time. Today, New Jersey property owners live under that same threat after the tragic *Kelo* decision by the U.S. Supreme Court gave government the right to take private property for anything they determined to be a public purpose, including development of property to gain the government more revenue.

Hardly a day goes by when there is not some tragic story of a homeowner or small business owner losing their property because some feckless politician joined forces with a politically connected contractor to conjure up a scheme to "improve" a neighborhood. This phenomenon scares residents from all walks of life in our state. There is a palpable perception that anyone, absolutely anyone, can fall prey to this insidious practice.

Republicans can reestablish the sacred institution of property rights by offering an amendment to the State Constitution establishing that the government cannot take private property for private development. This is simply returning to the original intent of the Constitution. I placed this exact ballot question before the voters of Bogota in 2004. The referendum passed 1408 to 293, an overwhelming message to Trenton, telling them just how voters feel about the use of eminent domain.

A statewide ballot question reestablishing property rights will galvanize voters to conservative principles, of which private property rights are the center. I predict this question will pass in every community in the state, including the poorest. In addition to galvanizing voters, this amendment will end the abuse of government power that threatens our future.

Since the nation's birth, the debate over our English language has been at the center of the preservation of our heritage of freedom and opportunity. English is the language of opportunity, the language of prosperity, and Republicans must muster the courage to weather the attacks of "racism" and stand tall on this vital issue. At the time of writing of this book, over half of all states have adopted English as the official language of their government. Republicans in New Jersey can place the same question on the ballot for the people of New Jersey to decide. With 85% of Americans agreeing English should be the official language of government, it will pass in New Jersey and end the debate once and for all.

Special interest lobbies have been laboring for years to undermine English as our national language and they have been using the power and money of government and our public schools to accomplish their goals. This must be stopped and conservative Republicans have the ability to do it right here in New Jersey, if they have the guts. Republicans should do away with the multi-million dollar boondoggle called bilingual education. This program is a failure that keeps thousands of Latino students languishing in Spanish speaking classes as much as six years. Even parents of Spanish speaking students know this and want their children to be fast tracked into English speaking classes.

English is critical to communicating the principles of conservatism. The language of conservative ideology cannot be translated into other languages without losing its meaning. The vision of our constitution and the immense individual liberty and opportunity that has resulted is inseparable from our language. Our view towards individual rights and privileges are shaped by the language by which those rights and privileges are defined. Republicans must overcome the fear of being called racists by screaming liberals and take a lesson from past leaders like James Madison and Theodore Roosevelt.

Throughout this book there has emerged one common theme - the growth of state government - as it becomes apparent that the state is not the answer to our problems - it is the problem. The not-so-invisible hand, the mysterious force behind the runaway expansion and diminishing of our rights has been the black-robed oligarchs of the State Supreme Court. This ultra-liberal judicial body has led the country in "progressive" decision making, ranging from the Mount Laurel Doctrine to interference in education to taking away our right to vote on debt.

The judicial branch of government is intended to be the weakest of the three branches, charged with the sacred responsibility of upholding the constitution and its safeguards against the inevitable intrusion of government into areas it should not be allowed to stray. I have referred to these unelected tyrants as black-robed oligarchs on more than one occasion. This gang has been allowed to exceed its authority by amending our constitution without voter approval, such as in the case of altering the debt limitation clause to suit their own agenda.

The pattern demonstrates, however, that perhaps the Court does not operate in this capacity without the tacit consent of the legislature and, even more so, the support of the Governor's Office. Many times, the Governor and legislative leaders have shrugged at the Court's radical orders, blaming the court for unpopular decisions and claiming their actions are out of their control. The court has in essence become another legislative branch of government, making the unpopular and destructive decisions the elected officials wanted but did not have the guts to tell the voters.

Republicans can take the majority as well as the Governor's Office by campaigning on a bold and decisive conservative platform and articulating a vision for our state's future. To deliver on that vision will require putting the Supreme Court in its place by amending the constitution to reestablish its original intent. The next step is to take back control of the legislative process by halting the practice of "legislating from the bench" and informing the Court that their power is limited to interpreting, and interpreting in a strict constructionist manner.

We are in the midst of a reordering of the political realities that have shaped our time. We know that the conservative principles the Republican Party has failed to uphold are at the base of the development of our state. The majority of New Jersey residents share the principles and values that lie at the heart of conservatism. Despite what some say, we are not the minority of the minority party, we are the majority of all New Jerseyans. Conservatism cuts across party lines, making up the majority of the Republican Party, a significant portion of the Democratic Party, and those self-described independents.

Conservatism means different things to those who call themselves conservatives. Pundits make a distinction between what we know as "social" conservatism and "fiscal" conservatism. The social issues - law and order, abortion, low income housing, quota systems - are usually associated with blue-collar, ethnic and religious groups, and normally aligned with the Democratic Party. The fiscal issues - income tax redistribution, high property taxes - are usually associated with the Republican Party members and independents who concentrate their attention on economic matters.

We must be willing to accept this view of two major areas of conservatism - or, better yet, if galvanized to the Republican Party, two different conservative constituencies. But at the same time, we should recognize that the old lines that once divided these two groups of conservatives are disappearing.

The time has come to present a plan of action based on political principle that can attract those committed to the "social" issues and those interested in "fiscal" issues. A winning combination is to combine the two major segments of conservatism into one politically influential team.

It is time to create a political coalition that will reflect the views of the great, hitherto unacknowledged, conservative majority. We went a long way toward doing it in 1993. We can do it again.

What we must strive for is not simply a joining of the two branches of conservatism into a temporary alliance, but the creation of a new, lasting majority, prepared to govern with a committed conservative agenda for New Jersey.

This will call for compromise. But, not a compromise of basic principle. Born of this coalition will be something new: something open and vital and dynamic, a movement the great conservative majority will recognize as the coalition that will determine the future, because at the heart of this undertaking is principled politics.

Conservative ideology has allowed itself to fall victim to being reduced to a stereotype image by the relentless diatribes of the liberal left. When they say something loud enough and long enough it begins to be considered fact. This has been the fate of the image of the conservative movement. Too often, in the press and the television evening news, it is treated as a call for "ideological purity." Whatever ideology may mean - and it seems to mean a variety of things, depending upon who is using it - it creates a picture of a stubborn, fanatical clinging to abstract theory. We have to recognize that, in this country, "ideology" is a scare word. And, for good reason. Collectivist socialism is, to give but one example, an ideology.

This is the complete opposite to principled conservatism. If there is any political viewpoint in this world which is free from slavish adherence to abstraction, it is conservatism. When a conservative states that the free market is the best mechanism ever devised by man to meet material needs, he is merely stating what a careful examination of the real world has taught us to be fact.

When a conservative says it is destructive to our economy for the government to spend more than it takes in, he is simply showing the same common sense that tells him to come in out of the rain.

When a conservative says that government-funded low income housing does not work, he is not appealing to some abstract theory of economics - he is merely reporting what he has seen throughout a history of failed government attempts, from the Soviet Union to the Newark Housing Projects.

When a conservative quotes Jefferson that government that is closest to the people is best, it is because he knows that Jefferson risked his life, his fortune and his sacred honor to make certain that what he and his fellow patriots learned from experience was not crushed by the doctrine of collectivism.

The fair and balanced efforts of ordinary men and women, working out their own lives in their own way - this is the heart of conservatism. When we conservatives say that we know something about political affairs and that what we know can be stated as principles, we are saying that the principles we hold dear are those that have been found, through experience, to be beneficial for individuals, for families and for communities - found through the often bitter testing of pain, and sacrifice.

One thing that must be made clear in this McGreevey-Corzine-Menendez era is this: The new conservative majority we represent is not based on abstract theorizing of the kind that turns off the American people, but on common sense, intelligence, reason, hard work, faith in God, and the guts to say: "Yes, there are things we do strongly believe in, that we are willing to live for, work for, and sacrifice for, just like those immigrant ancestors of whom we are so proud." That is not "ideological." It is what built this country and made it great.

Let us lay to rest the myth of a small group of ideological purists trying to capture a majority in a state that is "hopelessly liberal." Replace it with the reality of a majority determined to assert its rights against the tyranny of powerful union bosses, fashionable left-wing activists, economic illiterates who have commandeered elective office and the social engineers who dominate the dialogue and set the course in political and social affairs.

Our first challenge is to get this message across to those who share most of our principles. If we allow ourselves to be portrayed as ideological shock troops without correcting this error we are doing ourselves and our cause a disservice. Wherever and whenever we can, we should gently but firmly correct our political and media friends who have been perpetuating the myth of conservatism as a narrow ideology that cannot win in New jersey. Whatever the word may have meant in the past, today conservatism means principles evolving from experience and a belief in change when necessary, but not just for the sake of some social experiment. We cannot allow ourselves to be lab rats in Governor Jon Corzine's giant experimental laboratory.

Once we have established this message, the next question is: What will be the political vehicle by which the majority can assert its rights? I cannot agree with some of my friends who have answered that question by saying this state needs a third political party.

I respect that view and I know that those who have reached it have done so after years of frustration with the establishment Republican Party that has made conservatives so unwelcome. But the political success of the principles we believe in can best be achieved in the Republican Party. The Republican Party can hold and should provide the political mechanism through which the goals of the majority of New Jersey voters can be reached. The biggest single grouping of conservatives is to be found in that party.

It is more effective to build on that grouping than to break it up and start over. Rather than a third party, we should build a new Republican Party made up of those who share our principles.

The New Republican Party will not be, and cannot be, one limited to the country club, big business image that, for reasons both fair and unfair, it is burdened with today. The New Republican Party we must strive to create is going to have room for the man and the woman in the corporate office buildings, for the truck driver, for the cop on the beat, small business owners, and the thousands of New Jersey voters who may never have thought of joining our party before, but whose interests coincide with those represented by principled Republicans.

If we are to attract more working men and women of this great state, we will do so not by simply "making room" for them, but by making certain they have a say in what goes on in the party. The Democratic Party turned its back on the majority of suburban taxpayers and social conservatives. The New Republican Party must welcome them and engage them, not only as activists but as leaders and as candidates.

The time has come for Republicans to say to minority voters: "Look what we have to offer, we offer principles that African-Americans can, and do, support." We believe in jobs, real jobs; we believe in education guided by parents having a choice and available to all children, regardless of income; we believe in treating all Americans as individuals and not as stereotypes or voting blocs - and we believe that the long-range interest of minority Americans lies in looking at what each major party has to offer, and then deciding on the merits.

The New Republican Party is one that will aggressively seek out the best candidates for every elective office, candidates who not only agree with, but understand, and are willing to fight for a sound, honest economy, for the interests of our families and neighborhoods and communities. And these candidates must be able to communicate those principles to the American people in language they understand. The highest property taxes in the nation isn't a textbook problem. Friends and neighbors leaving the state isn't a textbook problem. They should be discussed in human terms.

Our candidates must be willing to communicate with every level of society, because the principles we espouse are universal and cut across traditional lines. In every legislative district, there should be a search for young men and women who share these principles and they should be brought into positions of leadership in the local Republican Party clubs.

We can find capable, articulate candidates if we offer a vision of leadership, and when we find them, we will begin to change the pathetic state of affairs that has led to a Democrat controlled state and the downward economic spiral they have created. We have to find tough, bright young men and women who are sick and tired of clichés and the pomposity and the mind-numbing economic idiocy of the liberals in Trenton.

It is at this point, however, that we come across a question that is really the essential one: What will be the basis of this Republican Party? To what set of values and principles can our candidates appeal? Where can voters who want to know where we stand look for guidance?

The vision was outlined in the 2004 platform of the Republican Party. This was not a document manufactured by insiders. It was hammered out in free and open debate among all those who care about our party and the principles it stands for.

The Republican platform is unique. It answers not only programmatic questions for the immediate future of the party but also provides a clear outline of the underlying principles upon which those programs are based.

The New Jersey Republican Party should use the Republican platform of 2004 as the major source from which a Declaration of Principles can be created and offered to the people of New Jersey. I make no claim to originality. This declaration is brief, derived primarily word for word from the Republican platform. It concerns itself with basic principles, not with specific solutions.

***

We, the members of the New Jersey Republican Party, believe that the preservation and enhancement of the values that strengthen and protect individual freedom, family life, communities and neighborhoods and the liberty and prosperity of our state should be at the heart of any legislative or political program presented to the residents of New Jersey. Toward that end, we, therefore, commit ourselves to the following propositions and offer them to each of our voters believing that the New Jersey Republican Party, based on such principles, will serve the interest of all the people of this great state.

We believe that liberty can be measured by how much freedom Americans have to make their own decisions, even their own mistakes. Government must step in when one's liberties impinge on one's neighbors. Government must protect constitutional rights, deal with other governments, and protect citizens from aggressors, assure equal opportunity, and be compassionate in caring for those citizens who are unable to care for themselves.

Our federal system of local-state-national government is designed to sort out on what level these actions should be taken. Those concerns of a state character - such as air and water pollution that do not respect community boundaries, or the state transportation system, or efforts to safeguard your civil liberties -- must, be handled on the national and state level.

As a general rule, however, we believe that government action should be taken first by the government that resides as close to you as possible.

We also believe that Americans, often acting

through voluntary organizations, should have the opportunity to solve many of the social problems of their communities. This spirit of freely helping others is uniquely American and should be encouraged in every way by government.

Families must continue to be the foundation of our nation.

Families - not government programs - are the best way to make sure our children are properly nurtured, our elderly are cared for, our cultural and spiritual heritages are perpetuated, our laws are observed and our values are preserved.

Thus it is imperative that our government's programs, actions, officials and social welfare institutions never be allowed to jeopardize the family. We fear the government may be powerful enough to destroy our families; we know that it is not powerful enough to replace them. The New Republican Party must be committed to working always in the interest of the American family.

Every dollar spent by government is a dollar earned by individuals. Government must always ask: Are your dollars being wisely spent? Can we afford it? Is it not better for the country to leave your dollars in your pocket?

Elected officials, their appointees, and government workers are expected to perform their public acts with honesty, openness, diligence, and special integrity.

Government must work for the goal of justice and the elimination of unfair practices, but no government has yet designed a more productive economic system or one which benefits as many people as the American free market system.

The beauty of our land is our legacy to our children. It must be protected by us so that they can pass it on intact to their children.

The time has come to bring about the great conservative majority party waiting to be created. To our friends who are now Republicans but who do not identify themselves as conservatives: I want the record to show that I do not view the new revitalized Republican Party as one based on a principle of exclusion. After all, you do not get to be a majority party by searching for groups you won't associate or work with. If we truly believe in our principles, we should sit down and talk. Talk with anyone, anywhere, at any time, if it means talking about the principles for the Republican Party. Conservatism is not a narrow ideology, nor is it the exclusive property of conservative activists.

Our task now is not to sell a philosophy, but to make the majority of New Jersey voters, who already share that philosophy, see that the revitalized conservative New Jersey Republican Party offers them a political home. We are not a cult; we are members of a majority. Let's act and talk like it.

Our party must be the party of the individual. It must not sell out the individual to cater to the group. No greater challenge faces our society today than ensuring that each one of us can maintain his dignity and his identity in an increasingly collective, centralized society.

The Republican Party must be based on the kind of leadership that provides a vision and takes its strength from the people. Any organization is only the product of the values of its members. A political party is an organization created to further a cause. The cause, the beliefs and the principles, not the organization, attracts and holds the members together. Our mission must be to rediscover, reassert, and reapply New Jersey's rich, independent heritage to our state and local affairs.

With God's help we will render up leaders with courage and conviction. Leaders who will draw their strength from those brave men who declared, "With a firm reliance on the protection of divine Providence, we mutually pledge to each other our Lives, our Fortunes and our sacred Honor."

We are living in a time when we must accept the challenge God has put before us or we will lose. It is up to all the people in the Republican Party to approach the challenges of today with real integrity. We are not just playing games with our own electoral victories - we are playing games with the survival of liberty and prosperity in our state. Those are games for which we will not be forgiven by future generations. The job is ours and the job must be done, if we are to preserve the freedom and prosperity of this state. If not by us, who? If not now, when?

***

We must make the solemn pledge to put our own self interests aside and put taxpayers first.

About Mayor Steve Lonegan

Steve Lonegan was born in Teaneck's Holy Name Hospital on April 27, 1956. He grew up and graduated from High School in Ridgefield Park where he set several high school track records. Steve earned a B.A. in Business Administration from William Paterson College where he was Football Team Captain and an All Conference Division Center, later earning an M.B.A. from Fairleigh Dickinson University.

Steve built and managed retail and manufacturing businesses employing dozens of workers and today is a custom homebuilder. He has served as state national finance vice president for the National Federation of Independent Business and is a member of the Knights of Columbus. He currently serves as Executive Director of Americans for Prosperity's New Jersey chapter.

Eleven years ago, overtaxed Bogota homeowners elected Steve Lonegan as Mayor and ended years of Democrat rule.

Town finances were in shambles. Taxes were skyrocketing, municipal debt was out of control and spending was going through the roof – far beyond the inflation rate and the homeowner's ability to pay.

Lonegan's "Taxpayers First" philosophy led to the elimination of wasteful and duplicative services, privatization of some functions and a more cost-efficient user-friendly government.

As a result, Lonegan's Republican Team has kept spending increases below inflation since 1995. The Lonegan Team has reduced debt and tax increases have been kept far below inflation in spite of massive state aid reductions to suburban towns like Bogota. None of the other 565 New Jersey Mayors can boast of such a record.

Thanks to Steve's strong, conservative leadership, Republicans kept council control for ELEVEN STRAIGHT ELECTIONS in a town that hasn't supported a Republican Presidential candidate in nearly 20 years. Lonegan was reelected in 2003 by an 18 point margin over his Democratic opponent.

Steve Lonegan led the fight against the Newark Arena taxpayer rip-off, challenged in court illegal state bonding that costs taxpayers billions and is a New Jersey's number one champion for the small business owner and the forgotten suburban middle class.

Mayor Lonegan led a successful effort to stop the McGreevey-Codey-Corzine Administration from forcing a Fifteen Cent per gallon gasoline tax increase on New Jersey motorists and has been vocal against any proposal to fund state government current expenses through long-term debt. Lonegan brought several lawsuits to stop state debt sold without voter approval. As a result a "Lonegan Disclaimer" now appears on all "contract debt" sold by state authorities saying that the State of New Jersey is not obligated to repay this debt and that bond buyers do so at their own risk.

Lonegan currently narrates the "Taxpayer Minute," a feature heard on radio stations in New York, New Jersey and Philadelphia and hosts a weekly radio show on WIBG in Ocean City. Lonegan has been a guest on numerous TV news programs including Your World with Neil Cavuto, Fox & Friends, Good Day New York, The Big Idea with Donny Deutsch, Glenn Beck, Hannity & Colmes, Scarborough Country and New Jersey Power and Politics. He is a featured columnist on PoliticsNJ. com and newspapers throughout New Jersey.

Whether it is speaking out for taxpayers, taking on state bureaucrats or fighting for homeowners, no one in New Jersey is as vocal, as active and as determined to succeed as Steve Lonegan. Tough and independent, Mayor Steve Lonegan's success can be attributed to three words "Putting Taxpayers First."

Married to the former Lorraine Rossi, Steve lives in Bogota with his daughters Brooke and Katherine. The Lonegan family attends St. Joseph's Roman Catholic Church in Bogota.

LaVergne, TN USA
13 January 2010
169850LV00003B/205/P